ADOPTION THERAPY

PERSPECTIVES FROM CLIENTS AND CLINICIANS ON PROCESSING AND HEALING POST-ADOPTION ISSUES

ADOPTION THERAPY

PERSPECTIVES FROM CLIENTS AND CLINICIANS ON PROCESSING AND HEALING POST-ADOPTION ISSUES

Anthology Edited By
Laura Dennis

Entourage Publishing
2014

Entourage Publishing
www.Entourage-Publishing.com
Redondo Beach, CA 90278

We would love your feedback! Send your comments to
laura@adoptedrealitymemoir.com
www.laura-dennis.com

Adoption Therapy
Perspectives from Clients and Clinicians on Processing and Healing
Post-Adoption Issues
Edited and compiled by: Laura Dennis

Entourage Publishing, Inc.
1st edition 2014 eISBN: 978-0-9856168-8-5
Paperback ISBN: 978-0-9856168-9-2

Cover Art by Linda Boulanger (2014)
telltalebookcovers.weebly.com

For Us,
And for the Next Generation

WHAT EXPERTS ARE SAYING ABOUT *ADOPTION THERAPY*

If you have a connection to, or any interest in the lifelong journey of adoption, this book is a must read. It should be in the office of any therapist who wants to be considered adoption competent and in the home of any adoptive family who wants to better understand the perspective of the child they are raising. Much of this book is told by adoptees. And as adoptive mom Lori Holden says in her Foreword ... "We should give temporary rest to our own thoughts ... to simply listen."

This intelligent, thoughtful book penetrated what I thought was an already deep understanding of the complexities of adoption. My book is marked up and tagged for future reference. Here are some of the golden nuggets that this book held for me:

"And the truth shall set you free."

"Sixty-five percent of clinical psychologists surveyed were unable to recall any courses addressing adoption in graduate school ... 85 percent in undergraduate coursework."

"Adoption therapy is like a delicate game of Jenga. We have to realize that moving one piece can tumble the tower or relieve the pressure that makes the next step easier."

"A therapist who expects gratitude for adoption is unlikely to understand the overwhelming loss that preceded adoption."

"My best tip for adoption education for both parents and professionals is to learn from those who have lived it."

"No feeling is your last feeling."

"The concept of a newborn as a blank slate ... persists so strongly in our culture that even the idea of newborn separation as trauma is virtually unrecognized within the psychotherapy field, let alone prenatal trauma."

"Secrecy in adoption was a social experiment that lasted for about fifty years ... and that is now recognized as contrary to the best interests to those involved."

"What wasn't talked about is often more important than what is."

I hope this book is read, shared and quoted widely among those in the adoption constellation and by the therapists who enter this world. Let's all listen and learn from those who are at the center of this experience.

Linda M. Schellentrager
Communications Manager, Adoption Network Cleveland, adoptive mom in a fully open adoption since 1992

* * *

Laura Dennis' anthology *Adoption Therapy* is a broad-reaching exploration of a wide range of clinical issues related to adoption. Dennis includes stories of pain and healing from adoptees as well as practical advice from therapists. Adult adoptees will realize that they are not alone, and will be given tips on what to look for in a therapist, if they choose to seek one. Therapists will have a guidebook to help them practice in an informed, competent, and non-pathologizing way. Whether you are an adult adoptee, a therapist, or both (or neither!) *Adoption Therapy* can be a valuable resource for helping adult adoptees live, as one of the authors writes, "with authenticity and integrity."

Addison Cooper, LCSW
Foster-Adoption Supervisor, Therapist, and founder, *Adoption at the Movies*
(www.adoptionlcsw.com)

* * *

The processes and pathways toward healing and wholeness are deeply personal and unique for every adoptee and adoptive family. This compendium shares the voices of healers, adoptees, and psychotherapists engaged in surfacing and supporting the wounds and traumas surrounding the adoption experience.

The essays and stories here share not only what has worked for some, more importantly how they came to discover what kind of support and treatment they most needed. Some engage in traditional talk therapy, some in peer support, some in somatic body work or primal pre-verbal modalities, and still others find a psychospiritual process to be their path toward self-acceptance.

In a world that offers precious little adoption competent therapeutic support, this book shares how some have found their way through the thickets of inadequate post-adoption services and the failures of the mental health system to find the supports that are right for them.

Martha Crawford, LCSW
Psychotherapist and writer,
WhataShrinkThinks.com

CONTENTS

ADOPTION THERAPY

PERSPECTIVES FROM CLIENTS AND CLINICIANS ON PROCESSING AND HEALING POST-ADOPTION ISSUES

EDITOR'S NOTE

By Laura Dennis

As those who are involved in the online adoption community—whether hoping to adopt, raising an adoptee, or advocating for adoptee rights and a voice for the adoptee experience (or some mix of these)—many of us have read about and even experienced firsthand the issues that adoptees have. The word, "issues," is perhaps a misnomer, a gross understatement, or a pale and withered description for very real psychological illnesses and emotional losses. Nevertheless, "post-adoption issues" is a catch-all phrase, and at least it avoids pathologizing adoptees.

The old thinking about adoption and mental health was: raise your adoptee as if she were your own. The belief that love and two adoptive parents were the only ingredients in healthy-adoptive-child-raising was pervasive, and continues to be in some circles. The new thinking—thanks to enlightened experts and more importantly, thanks to the voices of those who have lived this life—is that "as if she were your own" just won't cut it. It's easy to find passionate opinions on both sides of this debate, but I hope with books like these and others, the tide will begin to turn towards methods, approaches, strategies, and tactics for helping adoptees that give credence to the reality that raising an adoptee and children from foster care requires "something more."

What exactly that "something more" comprises is one of the primary questions of this anthology.

Throughout, you'll see our writers providing insight and possible solutions—drawn from personal and clinical experiences, and from peer-reviewed research. At the risk of having a "spoiler" right here at the beginning of the anthology, I feel compelled to share this book's amazing (but not surprising) theme with regard to the common denominators for healing:

> 1. An adoptee's first losses—including mother loss, heritage loss, ethnicity loss, language loss, and more—absolutely must not be discounted.

> 2. Whatever training or approach is used, the client's individual experiences must be validated through empathetic care.

(In case you may be wondering, yes, our writers do address those adoptees who do not *appear* to have experienced trauma.) Nevertheless, when I look at the above advice, it seems so simple ... and yet it's not. The stories you are about to read pierce to the very heart of one's being; they are raw and painful. But above all, the personal stories are honest; the clinicians are writing with the best-of-intentions.

To that end, among the seventeen contributors, thirteen are adoptees or had experience with foster care, three are adoptive parents (from domestic, international, and foster care adoption), and seven have advanced degrees in mental health. It's not insignificant that many of these professionals are adoptees themselves. There is something about the axiom "heal thyself," that perhaps draws adoptees into the field of mental health and wellness.

I am so incredibly proud to have such a well-educated, insightful group of experts gathered. In addition to giving voice to the adoption experience, it is vital that mental health professionals speak directly to their colleagues to educate them on the specific issues connected to adoption.

It's my hope that adoptees take this book in with them to their first therapy appointment, flip to one or two pertinent chapters and state clearly, "This. I need your help with this. My specific situation is a bit different, but can you help me with these particular feelings, these unhealthy behaviors, these post-adoption issues?"

On the flip side, the next time an adoptee walks into a professional's office, I hope that therapists, social workers, and mental health professionals hold these articles close to their hearts and keep the themes in mind. The insight and advice offered is invaluable.

* * *

Laura Dennis (Editor) was born and adopted in New Jersey and raised in Maryland. She earned a B.A. and M.F.A. in dance performance and choreography, with a certificate in critical theory. She gave up aches and pains and bloody feet to become a sales director for a biotech startup. Then with two children under the age of three, in 2010 she and her husband sought to simplify their lifestyle and escaped to his hometown, Belgrade. While the children learned Serbian in their cozy preschool, Laura recovered from sleep deprivation and wrote *Adopted Reality, A Memoir*, available on Amazon.

An adoptee activist in reunion, she writes at *The Lost Daughters, Adoption Voices Magazine* and her own blog, *Expat (Adoptee) Mommy*. Her essays have been published in *Lost Daughters: Writing Adoption from a Place of Empowerment and Peace*, and *The Perpetual Child, Dismantling the Stereotype*. Laura is passionate about giving voice to the adoptee experience and is proud to have edited the popular anthology, *Adoption Reunion in the Social Media Age* (Entourage Publishing).

FOREWORD

By Lori Holden

It's with a bit of trepidation and a great deal of humility that I compose the Foreword to *Adoption Therapy*. After all, you hold in your hand an extraordinary and incisive collection of writings about adoption and therapy, composed by many who have walked the long walk of facing trauma and healing from it. A majority of these contributors—and the editor herself—are adult adoptees.

Now if there's one thing adoptive parents are known for in adoption circles, it is for doing more than their share of the talking. Accurately or not, adoptive parents are seen by some as the moneyed ones in the adoption "triad." Accurately or not, adoptive parents are seen by some as the "winners" in adoption scenarios—they end up with their dreams answered while birth parents and adoptees suffer wounds that society doesn't recognize. Accurately or not, adoptive parents are seen by some as the ones with the voice, with influence to mold adoption law and policy to their benefit.

And adoptive parents have been accused of speaking about adoption issues when perhaps they should be listening.

Hence my trepidation.

This notion of listening is why I encourage adoptive parents like me—and others curious about the possible effects of adoption—to pick up this book and read it thoroughly. *We should be listening.* We should give a temporary rest to our own thoughts and feelings and suppositions about adoption and create within us an open space to simply listen.

The importance of being open

Being open to hearing a new point of view—maybe even a scary point of view—is an expansive state. Being open works best if one has healthy boundaries and appropriate permeability between self and not-self. It requires a healthy ego, one that doesn't need to "win" to survive, one that recognizes its inherent value and accords others the same recognition. Being open means you have less of a need to defend your truth than you have curiosity to hear another's.

Being open, however, does not mean there is no discernment. *After* creating space to hear others' truths, and *after* listening and trying to understand a different perspective, it's still all right to discern whether another person's truth fits into your own truths—or not. And even if you decide "not," it may be prudent to tuck away that perspective for a later time when your own evolving circumstances may cause you to look at the perspective again and anew.

As you turn these pages, I invite you to be open to the gifts and insights within, and to allow the possibility that not all chapters will look like gifts. Anything that strikes you strongly (and dare I say that could be every single powerful chapter?) is resonating for you, either positively or negatively charged, and indicates there is something there for you to look at—*within you and from your own experiences.*

Understanding neonatal trauma

As you read and understand, you'll find gems like these quotes that will help you better understand the experience of having been adopted:

> "To be conceived without being intended, to be carried in the womb of a stressed mother facing a crisis pregnancy, leave lifelong traces that persist without an understanding of their origins."

> "Adoptive families tend to seek help from a counselor three times more frequently than other families."

> "I felt like I was living under the terms and conditions of a contract I never signed."

> "Start early teaching kids that feelings are like clouds moving through. No feeling is your last feeling. Feelings are not permanent."

> "After a lifetime of stuck feelings, we are walking around with all of this baggage."

> "Our lives are a dance between knowing who we are as separate beings and knowing ourselves as parts of the whole."

> "Hyper-vigilance in children—frequently being in a 'red-alert' zone—is the result of some kind of trauma."

> On connecting with Nature: "Ida Rolf said that if you can't get it from your mother, get it from the Mother—the earth."

> "But moving on is much different from healing."

"It is possible to have the emotions without allowing them to control me."

"One classic example of 'parentification' would be an adoptive parent who constantly implores reassurance from the child that he/she is the 'real' parent.

On adoptee resilience: "We succeed not so much because of that original loss but in spite of it."

"What these therapy modalities have in common is the goal of resolving past trauma at the level of the body/mind connection."

Parents who adopted internationally may have been under the impression that a child would be nothing but grateful to the people who rescued him or her from abandonment or life in an orphanage. Surely it wouldn't be traumatic for these "lucky" ones to land in a loving home. It would be a good thing!

As a mom via domestic adoption, though, that last quoted passage struck me because once upon a time, people adopting newborns thought we'd bring into our homes a Blank Slate Baby. Because they were infants, these brand new humans would come to us with no problem that our love couldn't resolve. The babies didn't have words yet, so clearly they wouldn't have memories of their placement (which first involved a separation in order to make a new connection). Surely it wouldn't be traumatic for these little babies to go from a chaotic and unstable place into a family that longed for them. As with international adoption, it would be a good thing!

But I've come to know by listening to adoptees that *infants do know. Young children do know.* They may not know in their minds, in their brains, because it's unclear how we encode events that happen before we can do the encoding through words and thoughts.

But their bodies know. Their body/minds know. The bodies and body/minds of infants and young children who were placed for adoption experienced chemical and hormonal changes and responded with unique and complex emotions that got encoded and stored. Evidence shows that the body/mind houses every experience we've ever had, even those that are preverbal. What we are hearing from brain scientists, therapists and adoptees themselves is that *the memories of the trauma of a chaotic pregnancy and/or separation from source resides in the body/minds of adopted people.*

But what about resilience?

So why might one adoptee turn out even-keeled and unflappable while another is deemed a hot mess? If the "primal wound" is real, why isn't every single adoptee in therapy all the time?

We find the answer in the wisdom of Forrest Gump: Humans—like life itself—*are like a box of chocolates. You never know what you're gonna get.* Because of the infinite number of influences that go into making a person into who she is, because of the complexity of the interactions among those infinite influences from pre-birth on— because of the enormity of it all we can't identify any one thing that causes someone to be unflappable or a hot mess or anywhere in between.

Will your child be resilient? Who knows? It takes a lifetime to fully unwrap this metaphorical chocolate. Resilience and all other traits will emerge on their own timetables, being coaxed out or pruned based on life experiences and other factors. As your loved one's nature reveals itself to you, you can best respond by being open to who she is and attuning to that moment by moment.

Attunement and the adoptee

The longer I do this parenting gig, the more I hear from parenting experts about incorporating attunement. Attuned relationships mean we are in harmony with the other. Being attuned means we are willing and able to go into discord with our loved one, even when doing so is unpleasant and frightening. To be able to do this it helps to understand how others have handled such inner discord and come out on the other side.

I desire to be an attuned parent, however I'm finding though the journey is even more difficult than any other I've experienced. I bet anyone who loves an adopted person would like to be able to walk alongside her loved one and help bear the load of whatever he, or she, is going through. To do this we hold the intention to continually tune in with him, with her.

And to do this we must first hold the intention to tune in with ourselves.

As you turn the pages

So I ask you to open yourself to information and perspectives that may strike you as helpful, as scary, as possible solutions, as clues to a puzzle you're trying to figure out. I ask that you begin by preparing within you an open space to really listen to people who have walked this path—*before* you begin the process of discernment. I suggest that you monitor your own reactions to each chapter, and ask yourself probing questions at any time you notice a strong reaction (*why did that trigger me?*). I recommend that even if you discard the gist of a chapter today, that you remain open to reevaluating it another day.

May we all strive to open, to listen and to attune when it comes to adoption issues and the people who are faced with them.

* * *

Lori Holden writes regularly at *LavendarLuz.com* about parenting and living mindfully and is a columnist at *The Huffington Post* and at the *Denver Post*'s moms site. She is the author of *The Open-Hearted Way to Open Adoption: Helping Your Child Grow Up Whole*, written with her daughter's birth mom and after listening to adult adoptees and first parents tell of their varied experiences. She lives in Denver with her husband and two tweens and speaks to adoption agencies and their clients about openness in adoption and giving equal access for all citizens to original birth records. She has been known to practice the Both/And mindset when it comes to red wine and dark chocolate.

Chapter 1—"Untherapied" Adoption Wounds

By Karen Belanger

This piece is probably one of the toughest I've ever had to write. "Untherapied" is not a Webster's dictionary term, but it should be part of an adoptee's terminology because so many of us have struggled to cope with multiple adoption issues. To those who claim that adoption makes no difference in families, or is no different than biological families, I beg to differ. My adoption situation is an example of how the underlying issues of rejection, abuse, abandonment, and untherapied adoption wounds impact adoptee's lives in unexpected ways.

I remember being told I was adopted around the age of five. It came with a lot of questions unanswered. How could any child not wonder who the parents were that created them? Especially, when every other child around you was with his or her parents? What was the reason that the adoptee was not kept?

I grew up being told I was bad. Hearing, "No wonder your mother gave you away," only furthered my belief that inherently I was a bad seed who had been thrown away at birth. "You're just crazy," was an often-tossed-out phrase. Abuse, in the name of "spanking," including bruising, welts, marks, and being slapped were common. As hard as I tried to please my parents, I always fell short of most standards.

Around the age of eight I entered the bathroom, opened the medicine cabinet, and stared at the bottle of aspirin on the shelf wondering if taking all of it would kill me. It would take me years to realize that this is not normal behavior or thinking for an eight-year-old. But, neither was the world I was growing up in. Thus began my descent into the world of untherapied adoption wounds.

When I entered my teen years I began to accrue some knowledge about life, society, people in general and how they operated, along with bearing witness to the difference in treatment between me and the biological child of my adoptive parents. I was trying to put my finger on what was out-of-whack in my family situation, and how I could fix it. I picked up the pop psychology book from the library, *I'm OK, You're OK,* by Thomas Harris. It was a popular self-help book that attempted to give ordinary people effective coping tools to deal with the issues in their personal lives. Thus began my journey of trying to piece together the puzzle bits of my experiences into a healthy and coherent whole. I already knew from a young age that something was not "right," but I couldn't figure out exactly what that was. Worse, I believed it was my fault, mostly because I was told so.

I would go to extreme lengths and measures contorting myself into any shape or form I could to make certain I was acceptable in everyone's eyes. Having no sense of self or where I belonged, I tried to belong anywhere I could. My life became pretending, becoming a chameleon so as to be acceptable. What appeared to people externally about me was not the reality of what I was dealing with internally.

I was absolutely empty inside, a bottomless pit of need, self-loathing, and hatred. And, I hated myself for feeling that, too. Mostly, I hated my parents, I hated I couldn't seem to change anything, and I hated being adopted. And then I got really angry.

There were two emotions I lived between, fear and anger. Both existed just below the surface of my façade at all times. People mistook my fear for anxiety. They saw my anger and mistook it for my temperament.

They were neither. "She's high strung," people said to describe my moods. "Calm down," they said over-and-over in emotionally heated situations. I easily lost control and couldn't figure out why.

Then I discovered alcohol and drugs. Numb was better than feeling, and bad behavior became comfortable. Rebellious and anti-social behavior with significant others was even better because they validated it was okay, that you were okay, and the comfort of that—even if temporary, was well worth it. It was easier not to care about life, than to have to continually exert that much effort to try and succeed and always seem to fail.

However, the highs and lows of drugs and alcohol could easily trigger and fuel my underlying angst. As my tolerance grew higher and I consumed more, it also magnified my emotions, good or bad. Unfortunately, bad was VERY bad.

Violence played out in my relationships as it had in my childhood. I chose partners who abused me, and in turn, my anger over it gave me an excuse to act out against it. It wasn't simply anger, it was rage. I would scream and yell until I was hoarse and exhausted, throwing and breaking anything within reach. Then there was always the emotionally depressive hangover in the light of the next day facing what had transpired the previous night.

Fast forward a couple of decades plus through numerous relationships that disintegrated. I don't have to go into detail about all of them, because they were basically all the same relationship. Full of dysfunction, addiction, abuse, and headed towards an inevitable demise.

Along the way I had signed up with ALMA (Adoptees' Liberty Movement Association), one of the first adoptee search and activism groups around. I'd decided to try and connect with my biological parents, but I heard nothing back from the organization. Later, I would find out that I was a secret child and no one was looking for me.

I found John Bradshaw's PBS series on emotional and family health and watched, and then I read all of the books he had written that I could get my hands on at the local library. It was the first time I had considered the concepts of dysfunction, codependency, and the long term effect of abuse, anger, and rage. I learned about the huge impact those made on small children and the adults they would eventually become. I began to truly realize that what had happened to me in my childhood was still effecting me, and not in a small way, either.

I was growing weary of the emotional outbursts I could not control. The ups and the downs were draining. The disappointment I felt was continually overwhelming. But, I could not stop, and I did not know how.

Humor was always a great coping tool, and I used levity frequently in daily life. I remember I bought and wore-out a teeshirt that said, "I can go from zero to bitch in .05 seconds." Looking back now I see it as a subconscious statement more than it was a joke. I was wearing my heart on my sleeve.

I reentered college as a psychology major, with a vested interest of course in my own issues and healing, and signed up for a required course of adolescent child psychology. As I was reading through a chapter I saw, "Orphaned, neglected, and adopted children can often struggle with issues of rejection and abandonment." And there it was, in black-and-white print no less. The proof of what I had known all along: adoption had shaped and molded my life despite what anyone else had tried to tell me. It finally dawned on me how riddled I was with untherapied adoption wounds.

About the same time the marriage to my son's father landed us in mandatory state-ordered counseling for family violence. I had no idea the blessing this would turn out to be. I had won the counseling lottery as I was matched with an adoptive mother who was well-versed in adoption issues and trauma, search and support, and the importance of it all, not just as a professional but personally with her own adopted daughter.

As we progressed through several weeks of appointments with our counselor, issues became apparent and solutions to resolve them were given, discussed, and implemented. I remember distinctly in one session becoming angry over a remark my then-husband had made to me. Without forethought I lashed back, "You are cold, distant, and abusive. JUST like my FATHER!" There it was; I had done it again. I had made a choice in a partner based on my unresolved, untherapied adoption wounds; issues from my childhood.

Slowly the problems I had regarding being adopted came out. I remember jokingly saying one week, "I think I have double mother rejection syndrome." My counselor responded, "Yes Karen, you really do." Sometimes something posed in a comical way has a far less impact than facing the most important truth in your life head on. My counselor helped me to realize the underlying pain and loss I felt, the rejection and abandonment, and anger and rage I felt from being left by two sets of parents one physically, and the other emotionally. It was now clearly evident to me.

Although knowledge is power, old habits die hard. Knowing and doing are two separate subjects. I knew that I wanted to stop being angry and raging, I knew that my behavior was inexcusable, and I knew that these out-of-control emotions were taking a toll on me mentally and physically. The desire to heal myself became paramount. I had grown tired of being dependent on alcohol and drugs. It felt like a ball-and-chain around my ankle I had to drag with me every step I took. I slowly began to diminish the amounts I ingested. As I was becoming more and more sober, reality was becoming clearer and clearer.

I think the greatest wake-up call I had was becoming enraged one evening over my husband's addictive behavior(s). I smashed a glass on the night stand and sliced my pinky finger open. There was a great deal of blood. I hate blood as much as I hate doctors and hospitals. I refused to go. I believed it would be better the next day, in denial yet again. It was not.

I wrapped it and un-wrapped it and refused to really look at the depth of the damage, treated, and rewrapped it for several days. Finally I had to come to the realization that I had lost the full function of my little finger and without surgery at the very least, I would never regain it. I was a pianist and flutist teaching private lessons. My wrath had not hurt anyone else, thankfully, except for me.

The smallest hint of rejection, even if imagined in my fear-based psyche, could send me spiraling out-of-control. I would push, shove, and force people to the edge of leaving, then pull them back. Always testing and checking to see how loyal they would be in the end. Constantly waiting for the end, the finality, the time and day that I would be rejected again. Over and over I played out my unresolved and untherapied adoption wounds.

I was always hyper-sensitive. I could quickly become volatile and deadly with split- second knee-jerk reactions. Hurling objects within my grasp became my *modus operandi*. There was nothing sacred, and sometimes the things I loved most became the best objects to ruin. Photos, clothes, vases, I could be a tornado or like a seething volcano erupting on an irreversible path unstoppable even to myself.

CRASH!

"Screw you adoptive parents."

SMASH!

"Screw you biological parents who left me."

SLAM!

"Screw you universe or God or whoever put me here, punishing me undeservedly."

The lashing out and retaliation were in direct proportion to the untherapied adoption wounds bleeding over into every area of my life. I was emotionally hemorrhaging all over the place.

My best friend commented to me once, "Karen you are the nicest and the meanest person I have ever known." No truth could have been more evident to those who knew me. Normally, I was a kind, loving, helpful, and supportive friend. Popular and sought out for companionship, a shoulder to lean on, I was the friend who could always be counted on to be there for everyone. However, the other Karen—the one filled with bitterness and resentment when betrayed or deceived by those she loved—spewed forth venomous, vicious, demeaning accusations with relentless animosity upon any offender. There were dire consequences when you crossed the line with me. It was not very pretty.

I was continually shocked at the outbursts and seeming lack of control I had over these emotions. Constantly living feeling damaged beyond repair is no life at all. I earned my nickname "Crazy K." I felt like I needed to stand up in a room somewhere in a group and announce, "Hi, my name is Karen and I am a rage-aholic."

Finally with enough therapy and adoption counseling I realized that my life revolved around the deep relentless fear that I would never belong anywhere. That the facts were that I was not good enough to be a "forever person," and that I would never fit into the world around me. I was angry because I seemed to be left out, alone, with no place to consider home. Ostracized, abandoned, and rejected were my living, breathing world every day, whether I was consciously aware of it or not. Looking around at other people's lives and families, I was jealous of what they had that I did not, I was ashamed that for whatever reason I was not worthy enough of having it.

I've heard over and over that anger is a fear-based emotion and reaction. I believe it. The fear of being powerless as adoptees, of not understanding what happened to us, and that we never were and never will be good enough to be loved for who we really are, can consume us in our reactions and responses to life circumstances and events. We all react to anger in different ways by either suppressing it, becoming passive aggressive, living in denial, or lashing out as I did. None of it usually comes to any good. Eventually it snowballs into larger problems if not dealt with and resolved.

If certain behaviors are repeated they become patterns, and automatic reactions can get addictive. Even if the results are wrong, the reaction can often feel right. But we are not reacting necessarily to the current situation at hand. Rather we have triggered a much deeper emotion that has been trapped, pent up, shaken like an unopened bottle of soda. We are poised ready to explode.

Feeling compelled to act upon these now tapped-into emotions, there seems to be no "off" switch readily available, or a valve to at least slow the flow down. It's either fight or flight. We feel compelled to respond the way we usually respond, as if there is no other choice. Without realizing why we react the way we do, we've never learned there are other alternatives, new solutions to these ingrained emotional triggers.

We become stuck in survival modes of thinking and behaving. We become defensive, closed down, overly emotional, and live as perpetual victims. We indulge in escapist behaviors, and deep denial that adoption has affected us at all. Until we as adoptees can truly examine where these deep-seeded emotions stem from, and what in fact they mean to us individually, can there ever be any hope at all of getting our untherapied adoptee wounds under control permanently? Life can become very demanding and difficult with so many unresolved and unexamined feelings floating around inside of us just waiting for an outlet, the chance to be released.

An example is road rage that can result in seriously dangerous and sometimes even fatal circumstances. Certainly there has to be some underlying reason for people to react as uncontrollably as they do on a road or highway in an instant with a random stranger. Something had to have been set off for this collision course to have occurred. Same as with untherapied adoption wounds, adoptees carry with them such deep-seeded primal emotions that without a relief valve of some kind can easily and often turn detrimental to not only themselves, but to others as well.

There is so much pressure and expectation placed upon adoptees to fill the lives of adoptive parents and relieve their grief of not being able to have biological children of their own. Adoptees are, without question, supposed to live happily and gratefully in families where we share zero genetics and heredity. When we don't measure up to standards and expectations, many adoptees are then shamed, blamed, and further rejected. We are faulted for our own genetic tendencies, personalities, even down to our physical traits that are different. We are judged as either good or bad in direct proportion to our ability to satisfy the needs of others and these turn into untherapied adoption wounds that live within us.

With such a negative view of ourselves as adoptees our anger becomes a perpetual and a revolving door. When our basic emotional rights are ignored, ridiculed, and denounced, it also triggers the unfairness and injustice that has occurred in our lives we have endured yet can no longer accept. But what do we do with the anger from those limited parameters of emotions allowed us as adoptees and the expected gratefulness imposed upon us by the system of adoption, adoptive parents, and others?

Because adoptees have been taught to not trust our feelings, why should we trust our anger? We believe we are unjustified in our emotions towards what adoption has meant in our personal lives. Without a healthy outlet to express our fear, frustration, and pain, inner turmoil can mount and over time take a tremendous toll on our emotional, mental, and even physical health. Being chronically angry is exhausting. It can lead to self-harm, addiction, seclusion, chronic depression, dysfunctional relationships, and even suicide. I've witnessed and lived almost all of these.

When adoptees are told they aren't measuring up, or aren't good enough, it echoes the voices within our hearts and minds; that voice which tells us that our family of origin who gave us away must have thought so too. This must be the reason we are not worthy of unconditional love and acceptance. Some adoptees don't have to surmise these beliefs; they were stated to us as a matter of fact. These voices and self-talk become attitudes we carry about ourselves that shape who and what we are and become.

As adoptees and wounded individuals, we need to learn to be more tolerant and forgiving of our failures to control our emotions because there has been no handbook, or tutorial, or signpost along the road to show us the way. This in no manner excuses adoptees or anyone from bad behavior as a result of rage and anger. Self-forgiveness is a huge step in the right direction toward healing and the resolution of untherapied adoption wounds. Self-forgiveness reduces "fuel for the fire" and accordingly, the unacceptable actions resulting from those wounds.

But, being kind and patient with ourselves as adoptees can be more than difficult when we have grown up in our dysfunctional and unaccepting adoptive families. It's hard to spend a childhood surrounded by those who not only don't understand who we are as genetic individuals, but are obviously displeased with who and what we are. We become prone to people-pleasing tendencies, and we wear masks that cover up our true natures. We shove down deep our uniqueness. We doubt our talents and capabilities. This is a set-up to anger and rage down the line, when in sheer frustration our inner selves scream "enough is enough!" After we are intentionally or unintentionally emotionally injured by a loved one, by then it is far too late to suppress the mounting anger that turns into fury.

Fortunately, I was given some coping tools in therapy and one was writing. I had always enjoyed writing, what I found was that it was not simply for the pleasure of writing, but rather a primal instinct that flowed like Niagara Falls from mind to paper (or computer). Writing was and is amazingly cathartic. As I implemented more of the suggestions I received from my counselor, other adoptees, support groups, and writers, I began to slowly heal. One does not just change overnight after decades of abuse, turmoil, and confusion.

I still get angry. Everyone gets angry. It's a normal human emotional reaction. How we tend to our behavior when angry is key. There is never an excuse for violent behavior, no matter the reason or cause. I have awareness now where my anger stems from, and I am not ashamed when it comes up.

I utilize a three-step system when I am aware of the rush of a triggered adoption emotion. First, I realize that it is in fact an adoption trigger and that I don't have to respond immediately or react in any specific way until I have addressed the reason I am feeling the way I do. Second, I examine where these feelings are really coming from in relation to the persons and situation I am forced to confront. Am I being placed in a defensive position, rejected, unfairly judged, or being subjected to unwarranted criticism? All of these triggers from childhood that could easily set me off in the present. Third, I allow myself to feel what I feel: shamed, attacked, or belittled, I and wait for these feelings to subside without instantaneous action.

I have at my disposal positive coping mechanisms where poor decisions and bad behavior used to reign. I speak my mind passionately and confidently about how I feel without losing control. Working out, writing, reading, playing Mozart on a flute or Rachmaninoff on a piano, pulling out a knife and chopping the heck out of some vegetables and creating a culinary work of art, or digging in the earth planting and growing gardens are tools I have now. I have replaced the destructive tendencies that once governed my life. I found out my biology comes from musicians, dancers, cooks, and gardeners, so I now have these gifts and talents I inherited readily available to utilize in my daily life.

My specific tools are not what will work for others. That is the amazing part of being adopted and discovering your untherapied adoption wounds. We can then seek out and discover more about our original identities, unearth the talents and natural capabilities we inherited, and finally define and assert ourselves and our true identities in healthy and productive ways.

I admit I still test people. I put myself out there just as I am for people to "take it or leave it" right up front. Better to be rejected initially for who you really are, rather than being accepted temporarily for who you are not. Why invest yourself in a false relationship or friendship that you again will lose? I truly believe that's very much an adoptee characteristic and trait.

We are never done working out original loss and incorporating search and reunion into our lives. As adoptees we know all too well we can think we have mastered the anxiety and pain that plagues us. But when we least expect it, there it is yet again rising to the surface at the most inappropriate time, much to everyone's surprise, including our own. It is a work-in-progress, but it is always worth the effort.

Between the counseling, searching, the support groups, my writing, and the new information I have about my biological family, a great metamorphosis happened in my life. I no longer have to hide my authentic self away in a cocoon fearing further rejection from the world. Even my friends who had known me for years commented on what a changed person was. Addictive habits dropped away like shedding skin. I found a new found passion for life.

Adoption reform, activism, education, search and support replaced time-consuming wallowing in self-pity and hatred. Speaking and writing now fill my hours, instead of emptiness and isolation. I finally belong somewhere, but mostly now I belong to "me."

I look back on that poor, pathetic, broken child I was and grieve for the pain and confusion she felt growing up and into adulthood. It is necessary to examine our past and how it has molded and shaped us as the person we are today so we can set our course for the future. It is not right to base a child and adult's life on secrets and lies, and then hide the truth from us. It is not right for grown adopted adults to carry the weight and burdens adoption brings into our lives needlessly.

"And the truth shall set you free," has a greater meaning for adoptees. Adoptees deserve a life of wholeness and completeness, as much as is possible for any other human being. Adoptee voices, stories, and experiences matter and it long past due that adoption is discussed openly and honestly, not hidden beneath archaic laws, policies, practices, and belief systems. As I always say in regards to adoption, "If we teach our children to tell the truth, then first we must tell it to them."

* * *

Karen Belanger is an adult adoptee, the author of *Assembling Self,* an adoption poetry book, and writes at her blog of the same name. She contributes at *The Lost Daughters* blog and was recently included in the *Lost Daughters: Writing Adoption from a Place of Empowerment and Peace.* Karen has held various leadership positions within the adoption education, reform, and activism community over the past fifteen years. She is currently submitting pieces for two other adoption books and is working on her second book.

Chapter 2—Red Flags that a Potential Therapist Could Do More Harm Than Good

By Brooke Randolph, LMHC

Adoptive families tend to seek help from a counselor three times more frequently than other families. They seek treatment for behaviors that seem to interrupt attachment, social difficulties resulting from orphanage behaviors, neurological damage that may be caused prenatally or through abuse, trauma reactions, separation anxiety, other sensory deficits, or delays resulted from inconsistent, less than compassionate care. Often the stress alone of the major life changes associated with adoption that occur without warning to the child is enough to create emotional and behavioral concerns. Not all issues that adoptive families face are connected to adoption. Sometimes a child is simply bullied, but there are so many layers and complexities in adoption that can intersect with even these more straightforward issues.

Finding a competent therapist isn't just an issue for adoptive families seeking treatment for their children. When these children become adults and are able to fully process the depths of adoption, they will have more processing to do and new issues to face. As they proceed through various life milestones and developmental stages, adoption can take on new meaning or impact them in an entirely new way. Birth parents too have special concerns that are too frequently overlooked. Adoptive parents often have their own issues that must be addressed for them to be able to be the parent that their child needs them to be. Everyone involved with an adoption needs an experienced, competent counselor who can take the whole picture into account.

Most adoptive parents seem to realize that what works for most children, is not necessarily helpful for our kids. The same is true therapeutically in all adoption cases. Even when it comes to working with couples on relationship issues, years of one partner in the relationship feeling a little different and wondering where he or she fits means that certain ideas must be approached and addressed slightly differently than a therapist might address it with a couple where both partners were raised by their biological parents. Due to the numbers of adoptive families and adult adoptees seeking treatment and the need for specialization, it is disheartening that so many clinicians are grossly unprepared.

I cannot tell you how many times I have heard an adoptive parent say *we went to a therapist, but it only seemed to make it worse.* Adoptees seem to be gentler in their assessment that *it just didn't help,* or *the counselor didn't get it.* Sadly, it is much more common to hear these sentiments than it is to hear that a therapist was able to provide the support and guidance needed for an adoptive family or adoptee. As counselors, we want to work ourselves out of a job; we want our clients to come to a place where they no longer need us. While the circumstances and issues entwined with adoption often cannot be fully processed until adulthood, no child or family should be left struggling; there are understandings that can be found along the path that allow for the alleviation of distress if nothing else.

It is no wonder that so many therapists are making mistakes when trying to work with those who have been impacted by adoption. Most clinicians were never provided even a basic introduction to adoption, let alone an explanation or analysis of the complexities adoption entails. Sixty-five percent of clinical psychologists surveyed were unable to recall *any* courses addressing adoption in graduate school, which is better than the eighty-six percent who could not recall any courses addressing adoption in their undergraduate coursework, either (Javier, et al., 2006).

When asked how much time they spend discussing adoption in doctoral-level clinical programs, professors reported an average of 7.95 minutes per semester on adoption, yet they reported spending 22.17 minutes on the rare dissociative identity disorder, and 76.82 minutes for schizophrenia (Sass, et al., 2000). I have never seen a case of dissociative identity disorder, but foster care and adoption was something I dealt with at least weekly during my masters-level internship. Would you want your dentist to have spent ten times the amount of time in school on gum grafts as he or she did on cavities? Would you want your primary care physician to know the ins-and-outs of the rare blood disorder *polycythemia vera* rather than spending time becoming fully versed in blood pressure or diabetes? The medical community tends to embrace a concept that states "when one hears hoof beats—we think horses, not zebras," meaning the bulk of time should be spent becoming versed in those topics that they will encounter most frequently. If only psychologists and social workers took the same point of view.

Not only is there little-to-no training for most counselors, social workers, and psychologists, but many have only anecdotal experience with adoption. Most people can name a cousin or family friend who connects them to adoption, but every adoption situation is so very different that one connection provides little relevant information. The different types of adoption—foster care, domestic infant, kinship, international adoption— vary greatly in the process, people involved, and experiences of the child, yet even within each type there are innumerable variables so that no situation is exactly the same. Two families starting the international adoption process from the same country at the same time and both adopting children within the same age range can have vastly different experiences. Each child is unique. Some are more resilient. All have faced a variety of experiences unique to them. Each will express his or her stress slightly differently and each will learn individual coping and survival skills. Everyone whose family has been impacted by adoption knows the frustration of listening to someone's story about "this one adoption they know about"—whether a friend, neighbor, or second cousin, which likely has nothing in common with that family's experience. Anecdotal and personal experience is not enough to fully understand the expression of issues unique to adoption or the therapeutic needs of those impacted by adoption.

As a professional therapist, I have found that continuing education courses rarely challenge me. Most simply do not have the time to even begin to introduce the complexities involved with adoption. Seeking adoption competency through continuing education courses is unlikely to be sufficient. There are a few adoption competency trainings and special intensive courses that those of us who specialize in adoption would recommend, but until a practitioner is experienced with multiple cases of adoption, he or she may be unable to juggle the complex layers of developmental trauma, loss, attachment, etc.

We know we don't have enough training or experience, yet too many of us continue to see clients impacted by adoption—whether they are the children, the adults that grew up with adoption, the adoptive parents, or the birth family. Therapists who are not fully educated in adoption may not realize the damage their lack of experience can cause. In *Adopted Reality, A Memoir*, Laura Dennis shares about her reunion, and the paranoid delusion she found herself caught in merely four months later.

I was (mis)diagnosed with Bipolar I. In the two years of intense therapy that followed a horrible 51/50 stay at a psych ward, not one professional mentioned adoption, reunion, loss, abandonment, attachment, identity issues, or any combination thereof. It's my strong opinion that these well-meaning therapists completely missed the mark—addressing only the symptoms but not the cause. During the ensuing decade of pain and confusion, I struggled with relationships and mental stability. In a desperate attempt to avoid what would "assuredly" be a much worse breakdown, I regulated food, sleep, and exercise with, yes, near manic determination. It was only through writing and connecting with the fog-free adoption community that I've been able to process and heal.

Laura is an amazing, high-achieving mother, author, and advocate today. Still, I am sure she could have come out of the pain and confusion much more quickly if just one of her therapists had truly understood adoption issues. The clinician that doesn't get it exacerbates relationship issues, gives the child reasons to dig in his or her heels, and may even be prescribing unnecessary psychotropic medications. For more on the potential problems with working with a therapist who doesn't get it, refer to Jodi Haywood's writing, "Chapter 4—The Myth of Reactive Attachment Disorder."

Therapists who aren't prepared to work in adoption may not know to whom they can refer. They may not realize when it is appropriate and necessary to refer a client to an adoption specialist. They may be motivated to maintain their caseload or they may want to learn. I have yet to meet a counselor that does not truly want to help, but I have met several whose lack of personal insight or professional education have inhibited their ability to help the clients they see. It is essential that clients act as their own (or their child's) advocate in choosing a therapist, doing research, and asking tough questions. Be on the lookout for these red flags of therapists who could potentially do more harm than good.

Lack of additional training

Anyone who has worked in adoption knows that specializing in adoption means we have to have more than a general knowledge of many, many things that can impact a person, so we are able not only to peel back the layers, but understand how they interact. Adoption therapy is like a delicate game of Jenga. We have to realize that moving one piece can tumble the tower or relieve pressure that makes the next step easier.

Adoption is complicated. The emotions are complicated. The process is complicated. The developmental impacts are complicated. The loss is complicated. Training is essential. Keeping up with research and best practices is necessary. Learning the history of adoption and how people of different generations may have been impacted differently is important. Your therapist should be able to name trainings and conferences attended without hesitation. Some important areas your therapist should be familiar with include:

- Trust-Based Relational Interventions (TBRI),
- Theraplay,
- Eye Movement Desensitization and Reprocessing (EMDR),
- Adoption Competency Training (ACT), and
- ADOPTS.

Some of my favorite North American conferences for professional training include

- North American Council on Adoptable Children (NACAC) annual conference,
- Joint Council on International Children's Services (JCICS) annual child welfare symposium, and
- National Council for Adoption (NCFA).

There are also some great regional conferences I have attended including

- Adoption Knowledge Affiliates (AKA) in Austin and
- Adoptive Parents Committee (APC) in Brooklyn.

Less than one-third of case load includes adoption

While training is essential, true competency comes from experience applying knowledge and skills obtained from trainings attended. There is no hard rule for the minimum percent of a caseload needed for specialization. As a rule of thumb though, I think a third of a therapist's caseload should be individuals or families impacted by adoption to be considered an adoption specialist. Even if you do not believe your presenting problem is adoption related, it is helpful to have an adoption competent clinician to catch those details that may be interacting in ways you have not yet realized.

Sees a child individually

This is perhaps the biggest red flag for me, particularly at the initial session. There are many dangers with separating a child from adoptive parents as a part of therapy. Therapy is a unique relationship and experience. It is a one-sided, emotionally-intimate relationship where there is generally unconditional positive regard. The therapist acts as a vault for secrets, difficult emotions, and those things we imagine will cause others to reject us. It is easy for the therapist to become an attachment figure, but in adoptive families it is important that the adoptive parents be the primary attachment figures for the child. For this reason, family therapy is generally suggested for adoptive families. At times, I see only the parents and coach them in trying new techniques or learning to become the "primary therapist" for their child. Truly, I will never have more impact simply by seeing a child for an hour each week than involved parents will have. Educated, equipped, and empowered parents can make the most impact on a child's life. Ideally, the therapist will interview the parents first without the child even in the building. They can use this time to create a plan that is most appropriate for their family. There are some times, particularly with teenagers, that it is appropriate to meet with a child individually. However, if your first meeting with a counselor is separating children from parents, the clinician likely does not fully understand the dynamics of attachment and is not competent in adoption issues.

Does not ask for details and simply accepts, "I was adopted"

This may be a concern more common for those who were adopted themselves because adoptive parents are more likely to present adoption as significant to the concern. Whether adoption actually is part of your presenting problem or not, the details of your adoption are an important part of your psychosocial history. The age at which you were adopted, if it was kinship or infant or older child or inter-country or after foster care placement, and how you feel about adoption are all important to understanding your world view and developmental experience. Without this information, how

can your therapist help make links for you about
connections you may not have considered? Every
adoption is unique. A therapist that does not ask about
the individual's specific experience and outlook on
something so life altering probably does not understand
the full complexity of the adoptions experience.

Does not understand implicit memory (pre-verbal)

When asked about the worst thing a therapist
ever told her regarding adoption, one woman shared that
she was told, "We know that you cannot remember any
experience preverbal," thereby dismissing the importance
of her early life experiences. Infants exposed to violence
or other traumatic events will demonstrate trauma
reactions years later, even if they are not able to verbalize
the trigger for their feelings or reactions. A difficult or
stressful pregnancy is one of the risk factors for children
developing sensory deficits. Every life experience, even
those that occur before birth, plays an important part of
an individual's development.

In a study published in 2007 (Morris, et al., 2007),
toddlers who did not previously use color words were
shown that a bubble machine was activated when a
specific solution, identified only by color, was poured
into it. Two months later, these children were able to
identify the solution needed to activate the bubble
machine using the correct color word. Clearly the color of
solution that creates bubbles is not nearly as significant as
one's primary care giver, yet toddlers were able to recall
this information prior to using language. Recently, I met
an adoption professional who shared with me a story that
powerfully illustrates the power of these early memories.
During her trip to adopt a child, she wore a large-
brimmed hat to protect her face from the sun. When she
returned, she put the hat in the back of her closet and

forgot about it. One day, she walked into her room to see her teenage daughter (adopted well before developing language) sitting holding the hat. When her daughter saw her, she held up the hat to her mother and said, "This was from when you were scary to me." Her mother had had no idea that her daughter would have been able to remember any of their meeting or that first trip.

Babies are primed to recognize and bond with their biological mothers. It is commonly believed that breast milk transports flavors of the mother's diet to the infant. This is also true for the amniotic fluid, preparing infants to recognize their mothers and the foods of their culture and family group (Mennella, et al., 2001). Neuroscience researcher Shota Nishitani found that infants experienced less pain when exposed to just the smell of their mother's breast milk in comparison to the smell of breast milk from another woman, the smell of formula, or a control group (Nishitani, et al., 2009). Babies also learn the sound of the voices around them even before birth.

Babies born to mothers impacted by the tragedy of September 11, 2001, while pregnant, were found to have reduced levels of cortisol, and a vulnerability for developing Post-Traumatic Stress Disorder (PTSD) (Yehuda, et al., 2005). We know that in utero experiences not only prepare children for attachment, but they can drastically impact a child. A therapist who doesn't understand the impact of loss and trauma probably is going to be in over his or her head.

Talks negatively about family of origin or country of origin

We must remember that regardless of experiences, children generally idealize their biological family, especially if they do not have continued interactions with them. There are lots of good reasons for this. Even at a young age, kids seem to have an intuitive understanding of genetics and that biologically our parents are a part of who we are. They understand that there can be similarities in personality as well as appearance. I have watched children experience personal dissonance as a result of rejecting a parent's behavior, struggling to reckon their own value with how they value those who produced him or her. It protects mental health to have a positive opinion of one's parents because it makes it easier to have a positive opinion of oneself. The therapist must respect the child's origins as an essential foundation for self-concept.

One's opinion of one's parents can be the beginning of identity search and formation that takes on major significance in adolescence. This process is always complicated in adoption and often takes on importance much earlier as children try to determine if and where they fit-in their family, in their community, in their race, etc. Closed adoptions, transracial adoptions, inter-country adoptions—each of these can add to the layers of self the person who has been adopted must examine and figure out how to integrate. If the child or those around him or her has a negative opinion of any characteristic or detail related to the child's origin, this can complicate or interfere with the development of a healthy identity.

Even children that have been severely abused will still love and miss their family of origin. I find it to be a particular strength of character to love a person even when you reject his or her behavior—why would we try to encourage negative thoughts and feelings in children? Just because you have an acquaintance that you do not want to spend much time with does not mean that you think poorly of or reject that person.

Does not understand or allow for multiple attachments

Parents are able to love more than one child. Children are able to love two sets of grandparents. Why would we not allow a child to love more than one set of parents? This may be painful for the parents involved, but the therapist should understand the importance. While we do want the child to attach to the adoptive parents for the best interests of the child, I also believe that it is a developmental and emotional benefit for a child to have formed attachment to a biological/first parent. Perhaps the most emotionally healthy adoptee is the one who loves and is attached to both biological and adoptive families. When birth parents are not available for an ongoing relationship, it can be beneficial for children to stay in contact with a variety of biological family members. It can be a struggle for some adoptive parents not to feel slighted or jealous of having to share their child's love whether the relationship with the first family is ongoing or not. A therapist that is experienced with open adoption can share insights that can make this easier for adoptive parents, even helping those in closed or international adoptions where there is not ongoing interaction but the parents struggle with the memories and perception the child has of that first family.

Wants to give multiple diagnoses

Candidly, I am not a fan of diagnosis, particularly in cases of adoption.

Diagnosis is used as a quick explanation to communicate between health care providers regarding a cluster of symptoms and proper treatment for the condition. However, in counseling, much of the time, proper treatment and therapy is determined and executed between client and therapist solely without the involvement of other health care providers. You and your life story are bigger than the shorthand that diagnoses can provide. I want to work with individual clients, not vague diagnostic criteria (Randolph, 2011).

Diagnosis may be needed to help your child obtain certain services including an Individualized Education Plan (IEP). When multiple professionals are involved, it can be helpful to keep them on the same page. But there is danger in diagnosis as well.

A diagnosis of Major Depressive Disorder has been known to make it difficult-to-impossible to obtain life insurance, even when the diagnosis is more than a decade old. Other diagnoses might mean higher medical premiums (Randolph, 2011).

It is my opinion that the loss and complications involved in adoption are often more than enough for a person, especially a child, to have to manage. The potential long term consequences of diagnosis are concerning, but even more concerning is what diagnosis can do to a child immediately. Diagnosis can be perceived as indicating that there is something wrong with a person, that he or she needs to be repaired. It becomes a label that must be worked into personal identity. The response can be self-degradation, giving up, or taking on this label as identity. What diagnosis do you really want to be a part of you or your child's permanent record?

Beyond my skepticism regarding the benefits of diagnosis, I am always concerned when any child is labeled with multiple diagnoses. My bias on diagnosis is to find the simplest definition that encompasses the entire issue. Perhaps ADHD and Major Depressive Disorder and Oppositional Defiant Disorder (ODD) all apply, but it is likely that the symptoms expressed are all a result of trauma. One essential component of diagnosis is that for anything to be considered a disorder the distress must be in excess of what would be expected from the stressor. When the stressor involves separation from one's family and integration into a new family, a very high level of distress should be expected. For those who already have to deal with such loss and trauma, it seems even more important that we avoid giving them multiple labels that denote there might be something wrong with them. Many who have been adopted already wonder if they have some flaw. We should not be contributing to this concern.

Expects gratitude for adoption

While I believe that adoption can be wonderful and necessary for many children, it always involves loss. Children need families because they have been abused or abandoned, or their families do not have the means or support to be able to parent, or family members have died or become too ill to care for them. A therapist that expects gratitude for adoption is unlikely to understand the overwhelming loss that preceded adoption. Personally, I don't expect my son to be grateful that I adopted him; I expect him to be sad that he cannot be with his first family. Even children that love and securely attach to their adoptive families generally experience sadness or ambivalence that adoption was needed. While I still think it is a bit naive and self-centered for parents to expect or desire gratitude for adoption, they have the excuse of (hopefully) daily giving all of themselves to their children, contributing to this desire for gratitude.

Addresses behavioral concerns with punitive measures

Often the presenting problem that brings a family into counseling is some sort of acting-out behavior by the child. Generally though, these behaviors are merely a symptom of something else going on for the child. Children who have been adopted may have experienced early deficits of sensory experience, nurturing, food scarcity, trauma, loss, abuse, etc. Coming from these (and many other potential) hard places, means we must consider many other potential factors. It is unlikely that a child is simply pushing limits to determine where a boundary will be drawn. It is much more likely that he or she is in the midst of emotional processing, struggling due to developmental delays or undiagnosed allergies, or reacting to a history of trauma. If a child is not intentionally causing problems, firm, punitive measures are not likely to get positive results. Punitive measures also have the danger of interfering with attachment or unintentionally confirming the fears of the child that he or she is not good enough or isn't accepted or valued. These fears can cause things to spiral into more behavioral concerns. Firm punishment will stimulate natural defenses and make children more likely to "fight," ramping up the problem rather than solving it.

How to find an adoption-competent therapist

I strongly encourage adoptive families to ask their agency for a list of referrals as their first step. Occasionally families are afraid to talk to the agency about "problems," because they are concerned that they oversold themselves preparing for the adoption. We know that adoption is hard and requires advanced parenting skills. Even if you have some complaint against the agency you used, they are the most likely people to understand the needs your child has. You may also want to ask other adoptive families if they have had good experiences with a particular therapist. I encourage you to call or email first to ask questions that will help you consider if this particular therapist could be a good match for your family. The initial session should be for parents only—both a chance for parents to evaluate the therapist in person and for the therapist to help create a plan with you personalized for your family and your child's needs.

Similarly, the best way for adoptees to find an empathetic therapist is to ask friends who were adopted or the agency for a referral. Again, it is perfectly appropriate to call or email the therapist to ask questions ahead of time. If you are offended or put off, make it known. The therapist may have unintentionally parroted language he or she has heard previously, and he or she may be able to be very helpful if you are willing to correct or provide education about adoption.

When you're the therapist who doesn't get it

Awesome! If you are a therapist who has gotten this far and believe that you are not qualified to work with cases of adoption for one or several of the reasons above then you have the ability to make an honest self-assessment. You have two choices: you can seek out adoption competency or you can start referring. If you aren't ready to refer all of your cases related to adoption to a qualified expert, then please immediately seek supervision or mentorship from an adoption specialist. Remember the essential edict for all helping professions, *primum non nocere*, first do no harm. To ensure that you are not unintentionally one of the many therapists who have "made it worse" according to so many adoptive families and adoptees, you will need to carefully review your adoption cases with a qualified professional.

The next step is to start seeking out all the additional trainings that you can. You will likely receive continuing education credit for these courses, which include:

- The Training for Adoption Competency from the Center for Adoption Support and Education (C.A.S.E.) is a good place to start.
- National Council for Adoption offers free, online Pregnancy Counseling Training, which is another good introduction to adoption and awareness of all parties involved; they also offer other valuable webinars.
- Adoption Learning Partners can provide an introduction through their range of webinars for professionals.
- Creating a Family offers online learning through a weekly radio program, blogs, and videos.
- Or, find an agency locally who offers education and ask if you can participate in their program as well.
- I also strongly recommend Trust-Based Relational Interventions (TBRI) training from Texas Christian University. In fact, I look first for TBRI trained therapists when helping clients outside of Indiana find a counselor in their area if I have not specifically met or received a referral from someone I trust.

Attending trainings is important, but if you are not constantly working with a variety of different cases, it is easy to forget the details of the trainings or how widely varied adoption cases can be. You will remember what applies to the clients with whom you work, but you may potentially forget things that could be much more common and important to new clients.

There is a plethora of adoption books that can help expand your knowledge base. I would recommend the following books for a general education on adoption:

- *The Connected Child* by Karyn Purvis, David Cross, and Wendy Sunshine;
- *The Boy That Was Raised As A Dog* by Bruce Perry;

- *Telling the Truth to Your Adopted or Foster Child* by Betsy Keefer and Jayne Schooler;
- *Inside Transracial Adoption* by Beth Hall and Gail Steinberg,
- *The Out-of-Sync Child* by Carol Stock Kranowitz,
- *In On It* by Elisabeth O'Toole,
- *Theraplay: Helping Parents and Children Build Better Relationships Thorough Attachment-Based Play* by Phyllis Booth and Ann Jernberg, and
- *My Family, A Symphony; A Memoir of Global Adoption* by Aaron Eske.
- The Donaldson Adoption Institute is also a wonderful source for up-to-date research and education.

This is simply a place to start. Each individual or family you work with will require individual research.

My best tip for adoption education for both parents and professionals is to learn from those who have lived it. Every story is unique, so your *one friend that was adopted* does not actually give you a good understanding of how adoption impacts an individual from childhood through adulthood. I have listened to or read the stories of hundreds of adoptees and no two are the same. There are some similarities, but as with most things there are more differences within groups than differences between groups. This book is a compilation of adoptees with different stories. I am privileged to be able to consult with them and hear their stories. I purposefully seek out those who have lived adoption and I have a standing offer to buy coffee for anyone willing to sit down with me and share from their experience. I certainly encourage you to adopt a similar policy.

References

Dennis, Laura. *Adopted Reality, A Memoir* (Redondo Beach, CA: Entourage Publishing, 2014).

Javier, Rafael Art, Amanda L. Baden, Frank A. Biafora, and Alina Camacho-Gingerich. *Handbook of Adoption: Implications for Researchers, Practitioners, and Families* (Thousand Oaks, CA: Sage Publications, 2006).

Mennella, Julie A., Coren P. Jagnow, and Gary K. Beauchamp. "Prenatal and postnatal flavor learning by human infants," in *Pediatrics*, 107 (6): e88. DOI: 10.1542.

Morris, Gwynn and Lynne Baker-Ward. "Fragile But Real: Children's Capacity to Use Newly Acquired Words to Convey Preverbal Memories," in *Child Development*, 78: 448–458. DOI: 10.1111/j.1467-8624.2007.01008.x.

Nishitani, Shota, Tsunetake Miyamura, Masato Tagawa, Muneichiro Sumi, Ryuta Takase, Kirokazu Doi, Hiroyuki Moriuchi, and Kazuyuki Shinohara. "The calming effect of a maternal breast milk odor on the human newborn infant," in *Neuroscience Research*, 63: 66-71. DOI: 10.1016/j.neures.2008.10.007.

Randolph, Brooke. "How Insurance Inhibits Good Therapy" *Brooke Randolph* blog, March 10, 2011, http://brooke-randolph.com/Blog/How_Insurance_Inhibits_Good_Therapy.

Sass, Daniel A. and Douglas B. Henderson. "Adoption Issues: Preparation of Psychologists and an Evaluation of the Need for Continuing Education," in *Journal of Social Distress and the Homeless*, 9 (4): 349-359. DOI: 10.1023/A:1009497927928.

Yehuda, Rachel, Stephanie Mulherin Engel, Sarah R. Brand, Jonathan Seckl, Sue M. Marcus, and Gertrud S. Berkowitz. "Transgenerational Effects of Posttraumatic Stress Disorder in Babies of Mothers Exposed to the World Trade Center Attacks during Pregnancy," in *The Journal of Clinical Endocrinology & Metabolism*, 90 (7): 4115-4118. DOI: 10.1210/jc.2005-0550.

* * *

Brooke Randolph, LMHC, is a parent, therapist, and adoption professional with more than twenty years of experience working with children and families. She is a private practice counselor in Indianapolis, Indiana; the Vice President of PR, Outreach, and Communications at KidsFirst Adoption Services; and the mental health expert contributor at *DietsInReview.com*, a national diet and fitness column. She was a founding member of MLJ Adoptions, Inc., where she served as the VP of Social Services for seven years. She is a member of the Young Professionals Advisory Board for The Villages of Indiana, Inc., a child and family services agency that serves over 1,400 children and their families each day. She adopted an older child internationally as a single woman, which she considers one of the most difficult and most rewarding things she has ever done. She has authored adoption education materials and presented at numerous conferences and workshops throughout North America. Brooke is primarily motivated to encourage, equip, and empower parents and individuals to make changes that strengthen their lives, their careers, and their families.

Chapter 3—Approaches for Repairing the Wounds of Separation

By Rebecca Hawkes and Suzanne Schecker, Ed.D, LMHC

*R*ebecca Hawkes is an adult adoptee, an adoptive parent by way of foster-care adoption, and a certified trauma-informed parenting instructor. *Suzanne Schecker is a psychotherapist with a focus on trauma and mindfulness who experienced her own separation from family as a young girl in an informal foster care arrangement. Suzanne also lives in an intentional multi-generational community called Treehouse Community, created to support foster families. Rebecca and Suzanne met through their involvement in the Re-Envisioning Foster Care in America movement and sat down together to have the following conversation for this book:*

Rebecca—In your bio on your website, SuzanneSchecker.com, you wrote, "All of my work, whether with the individual or the larger community, has been about healing the wounds of separation; of bringing together the parts that have been scattered and separated."

This seems like a perfect jumping off place for a discussion about adoption and foster care. One of the challenges that adoptees and foster children or former foster children sometimes face in a therapeutic setting is that there is not always a full acknowledgement of those wounds of separation. I'm wondering if you could start by talking about why it's so important for adoptees, and others, to bring together the parts that have been scattered and separated?

Suzanne—I feel strongly that one of our very most basic human needs is belonging. Family is a form of community and it comes with ancestors; it comes with history; it comes with historical context; it comes with a whole community of people that live in one's neighborhood or town. When you remove children from their parents, you're removing them from all of that, from the entire extended context of family and community that they were born into. Their extended family is gone. The smells and sounds and feel of their neighborhood are gone. When you remove children from their families, you're tearing them out of their roots, out of the very foundation of their being. You're not just removing the child from one particular unskilled parent who, for whatever reason, wasn't able to parent at the moment.

Those children grieve. They go into a deep, deep sense of grief for that loss. And they feel alien. They're going someplace where they don't recognize the smells or the feel of the people or the sound around them. Especially if they're little, they've lost their points of reference. Children are absolutely grieving when they're removed from their family. And there's nothing neurotic or mentally ill about it; it's just our human nature. It's just a normal response to being taken away from the core of one's foundation in this world. I feel very strongly about that, and I think that so much of the work that we do as therapists is repairing that original rent.

Separation from family tears the soul open. People don't realize that in my profession. I used to teach child development and even in developmental psychology there's very little that combines the spiritual and the scientific biological roots with the psychological wellbeing of children. I think all of this comes together in kind of a gestalt of safety, and when a child loses that sense of safety and belonging, it follows the child throughout the lifetime. And it's not that children aren't very flexible and adaptive and capable of bonding to new people and feeling at home in new situations, but that early separation will always be a part of who they are. It's not necessarily going to destroy their lives. I think eventually it can actually strengthen and add to their ability to be compassionate people in the world because they know what it's like to have one's heartbroken so very early.

Rebecca—It's what my adoptee friends and I sometime refer to as "adoptee resilience." We succeed not so much because of that original loss but in spite of it and in some ways through overcoming and through healing.

Suzanne—Right. I mean, in my own life I've known a separation from my mom. She made a kind of unofficial foster home for us because she was a single mom who had to work and found a home to board us for five or six years. She would visit us there and I remember I had a similar kind of heartbreak. This was the person I loved most in the world and she was no longer a part of my daily life, and that broke my heart in a way that I think is similar to what happens in more formalized separations. I spent a lifetime trying to heal that separation. Eventually, I grew to a point where I realized that everybody's heart gets broken in different ways. We move through it because when hearts get broken they get stronger and more compassionate.

And then if we look at this issue of separation through a larger point of view of people around the world—if we look at it historically and consider children who are ripped from their families during war and separated for a million really painful reasons—it's amazing what the human soul can survive.

Rebecca—Your last comment reminds me of an adoptee writer named Daniel Ibn Zayd who has helped me understand adoption within the broader context of other groups of people who've been displaced, to see those connections.

Suzanne—Yeah, oh sure. Look at people who have been separated because of genocides and people in refugee camps. It's huge, and it's all similar, being disconnected from your culture, from your roots.

Rebecca—I think some of what happens in adoption—and specifically adoption within a therapy context—is that professionals, parents, and others don't always understand that the child who is displaced by adoption or foster care experiences all these things also, even though they end up, perhaps, in a loving replacement family. There is a gain but also still a loss.

Suzanne—Absolutely.

Rebecca—One effect of separation in some adoptees and foster children is a tendency toward hyper-alertness. Foster children especially may carry high levels of stress that tend to push them more easily into a "red-alert" zone in which the body is telling them that there is danger. On your website you define mindfulness as focusing awareness on the breath and you point out that we can learn to be present in our bodies and witness the thoughts, sensations and emotions that move through us. Can you talk a little about this or other aspects of your work that relate to the intense thoughts, sensations, and emotions that foster and adoptive children may experience?

Suzanne—Yes, you mention children who are hyper-vigilant and usually hyper-vigilance is the result of some kind of trauma, and trauma as far as I'm concerned includes separation from those we love. It may seem counterintuitive, but there is actually some research that mindfulness practice does work with anxiety. There's a considerable and growing amount of research supporting the assertion that we can manage fear and a certain amount of pain and distress if we can train ourselves to sit still and trust that we can manage it all. Fear, pain, and distress are part of being human. Stress is a part of the human experience that everybody has at one time or another, to different degrees. It can be helpful to teach children to not immediately run away from it and go to something else that's going to numb those feelings.

So yes, some kind of mindfulness practice can be very helpful. I don't expect two-year-olds to sit still and watch their breath, but you can begin to train children in a general way at a very young age. I remember when I would go to visit my grandmother as a kid. After lunch, there was a walk. Everyone in the family went for a walk, and when we came back from the walk, it was nap time. You didn't have to sleep, but you had to go to your bed and you had to be quiet. You could read. You could think. You could stare out the window. But it was kind of an early introduction to the notion of quiet, peaceful, contemplative time as part of everyday life. If you were at their house and it was three o'clock, it was naptime for an hour. And I loved it; I absolutely loved it. It made me feel like I was given this skill of self-regulation. I was taught how to self-regulate, and we can teach children that.

Rebecca—That's so interesting to me, because I just recently read an article about something called Head Start Trauma Smart. It's a program in which preschool children who have experienced trauma are taught to use breathing and other techniques to regulate themselves. The underlying idea that, yes, we can teach children calming, regulating skills—which leads me to my next question. In addition to naptime or quiet time, do you have other suggestions for helping children, and others, self-regulate?

Suzanne—One thing you can do is to start early teaching kids that feelings are like clouds moving through. No feeling is your last feeling. Feelings are not permanent. If you feel really sad, you have a good cry, you feel better afterwards, just like the sun comes out after a good rain. If children know that, then they know that they are not going to drown in that feeling. You have to comfort children when they are in fear because that's probably the last thing they can regulate when they are little, but even with fear, children can find a way. They will find some kind of creative solution if you don't hand it to them, if you begin to suggest that that there are all of these possibilities to deal with feelings.

Rebecca—One of the things I did with my daughter when she first moved in were some exercises from Peter Levine, who does Somatic Experiencing. He has a book called *Trauma Proofing your Kids* that had some exercises in which the child pretends that he or she is an animal in danger. The child is guided to imagine themselves, as the animal, escaping to a safe place and then release the traumatic energy of the flight to safety. It seemed helpful to bring her awareness to her body sensations and through a story train her to move beyond the initial traumatic experience.

Suzanne—Yes, that's powerful. Another thing that comes to mind is neuro-feedback, which is done with a computer. It's absolutely wonderful for children. They sit at a computer and their brain levels are measured. Using the computer they can actually observe and regulate some of their own body functions, and by doing that they can actually learn to relax when they are extremely anxious or are having a panic attack or are frightened of something. They also learn to observe their breath and regulate though breathing.

Rebecca—Because with the feedback from the computer they are learning to recognize what it feels like when they are in a calm and regulated state?

Suzanne—Right. And they are able to learn that they can do something from inside themselves that changes it, which is pretty amazing. They are learning that they have control.

Rebecca—I read a blog post recently that was focused on helping foster children heal. The author used the metaphor of a stream as "that still, quiet place where we find our balance, center ourselves, and cleanse away our hurts." She went on to say, "Foster children need the opportunity to be children again, and they need help finding healing waters. They need to feel the splash of a puddle, the cleansing of the water. They need to hear the sound of the brook to remind them that they are still alive. They need something to help them find their balance" (Phillips, 2014).

It seems to me that this concept overlaps with some of what you've been saying about mindfulness. Whether it's by sitting at a computer or taking a quiet time, children (and adults, too) need to find ways to come to balance, to come to regulation.

Suzanne—I love that metaphor that for a lot of reasons. I love it because it connects children with nature and shows the interconnectedness of this whole world that we live in. Also, water represents emotions. I love the idea of a stream because a stream flows. It's an experience of impermanence, which is really one of the foundational principles of mindfulness. This idea that we're all just moving through here, that all of life is a flow.

Rebecca—And when we're in flow and able to let the emotions and sensations flow through us, rather than resisting, we're in a more harmonious place?

Suzanne—Yes. I studied something called Wave Work, created by Dayashakti, and it was a similar concept. Our emotions rise from our belly and move like a wave. They arrive and increase in intensity, and then they crest. And on the other side of the crest, they get integrated. Sometimes there's an ah-ha moment. Imagine a little child who falls down and scrapes a knee. The child may make a series of sharp inhalations. You can actually see the emotion increase and the child screams and cries and then is done. They look around and see that they're okay and they are off to do something else. The emotion has been allowed to complete itself and the experience is integrated.

Rebecca—I'm reminded again of Peter Levine, who writes about how animals in nature after they are attacked will tremble and shake it off, literally. But humans, as we move into adulthood, seem to lose that ability.

Suzanne—Yes, because we are taught to cut that wave off. People have told us not to be a cry baby. People have taught us, along the way to adulthood, not to allow the completion of that cycle. And so it never gets fully integrated. Then we're holding on to it. We move on, but the emotion is stuck. After a lifetime of stuck feelings, we are walking around with all of this baggage. And then it gets triggered. Somebody looks at us the wrong way and something from twenty-years-ago gets triggered and we're yelling and we don't know why.

Rebecca—Absolutely. Whereas, the more we can learn as children, and even as adults, to process those emotions as they come up, the less we end up carrying around with us.

For me, the trauma of separation happened as an infant. It was pre-verbal, which doesn't necessarily make it any easier to heal from. On the other hand, children who come into foster care at an older age may have clear memories of times when their parents were, for whatever reason, unable to parent effectively. In the worst cases, they may have memories of neglect and abuse. But whatever the circumstances, we need to find a way to heal. Often that means healing the relationship, as well as the individual.

Suzanne—I agree, and we also need to find a way to shake the core "I'm not loveable" belief that sets in when your parent leaves you, for whatever reason. People go through life believing, "There must be something wrong with me that I'm not loveable," and that is really hard. I do EMDR (Eye Movement Desensitization and Reprocessing), and I see that belief removed sometimes in people who are seventy-years-old. It can take a whole lifetime to get rid of that belief because it's so deeply embedded.

Rebecca—On your website you describe the work of therapy as "reconnecting the parts of ourselves that feel isolated and split off from others." You also live in an intentional multi-generational community created to support foster families and have an interest in the ways individuals can be supported by community. What do you view as some of the therapeutic/healing benefits of community? Do you think community is of special importance to adoptees and foster children?

Suzanne—I'm a community person. I've lived in community for long periods of my life and alternated that with living alone. I also need periods of quiet contemplation on my own. I think our lives are kind of a dance between knowing who we are as separate beings and knowing ourselves as parts of the whole. I think of the analogy in physics of light that manifests as both particles and waves. We are molecules of light and water; part of one big ocean, but also individual drops of water or particles of light. We're meant to sparkle as individual particles but not to lose our identity as a part of the whole. There is this wondrous dance between these two ways of being in the world that we all experience.

I think in our culture in particular, it can be so hard to experience our own personal identity and shine as an individual when we don't know ourselves as part of a larger whole. We need that connection to others because it is in the reflection of others that we can know ourselves. Community gives that connectedness to everybody who's a part of it. I have learned so much from being here in this community. I've watched the kids thrive from being here. They know we are here. They know they can go to any house and say, "Can I use your phone?" or "I need to talk," and they'll be invited in and given a glass of milk and cookies. Somebody will listen to them. Maybe it's a fantasy, but that's part of how I think the world used to be. I think especially for kids who have been separated from their families, community can give back a sense of belonging and of family. It may not be their biological family. It might not heal that early wound totally, but they have a sense of belonging somewhere.

Rebecca—Wow, I love that you brought up the conflicting pulls of the need for togetherness and belonging versus the need for alone-time and ways of defining as an individual. I went to a yoga class recently that was focused on the themes of inclusion and exclusion. The yoga teacher had us at times turning away from the group and doing poses on our own, which represented those times we go away from community, and at other times she directed us to turn and face the group in a circle. We even did supported postures altogether as a group. It was a perfect metaphor. It's so interesting to me that you went there because the very next question that I have here to ask you is this: I think that in myself and others I sometimes see a pattern of pulling away from community at times, as you mentioned, pulling inward for purposes of self-protection or for healing, alternating with periods of re-integration into community. Adoptees and foster children sometimes present with behaviors that others interpret as anti-social, but there's really more going on than meets the eye. Do you have any thoughts on this, on the idea of retreating from and re-integrating into community and why that can be necessary sometimes?

Suzanne—I think children who have been abandoned or abused can find it scary to get too close to people too quickly, and they need to pull back and develop their inner resources for a while. It's hard to judge because we don't ever really know what goes on inside anybody else. I know there are some behaviors that some foster and adoptive children have that are self-protective. People they've opened their hearts to in the past failed them or left them, so it's harder for them to trust. Sometimes, part of not being able to trust is misinterpreting things, being super sensitive and taking things too personally. I know I was the kind of kid that would easily misinterpret the slightest thing as something that was my fault or something that was about me when it had nothing to do with me at all. That's a big part of doing therapy with children. I've worked some with adolescents, and I see adolescent girls in particular make that mistake. Some interpret everything in terms of, "Do you like me or do you not like me?"

I think part of what we have to teach children, gently, is that not everything is about them. Not in a judgmental way, but so that kids can begin to expand their sense of knowing how other people respond to things. Going back to mindfulness, I think if we spend some time developing a sense of our own inner being— our connection with our personal selves and our connection with the greater whole—over time we look less and less outside of ourselves to define who we are. We no longer take other people's opinions of ourselves as seriously. It becomes less and less important because you begin to develop your own sense of who you are. And when you are doing something, whether skillful or not, you accept yourself. I love the Buddhist theory that the worst you can ever do is be unskillful. I love that because it's a gentle knowing.

You can teach children to laugh at themselves when they make mistakes and to let it go and to not define people and themselves by their mistakes. It comes down to a kind of generosity of heart, to helping kids touch into their own innate kindness. If they see that kindness in themselves, then they can extend that to other people. If someone is mean to them, they can see that it's not personal. I think a big part of what therapy can do is practical everyday reflecting.

Rebecca—I think that that sense of "it's not all about me" and "it's not all directed at me" is something that a lot of us come to understand as we get older, but maybe there are ways to introduce those concepts to children and teenagers. Or even later in life, to start thinking more about these kinds of things.

Suzanne—Absolutely. And foster kids may need it earlier and with a little more specificity and direction because it's natural that they interpret things as their fault that they lost their family. Because that's what kids do. They blame themselves. It's too hard to assume that our parents aren't capable of being parents. It's easier for children to blame themselves because then they figure they can do better. They think, "If I get better, maybe they'll love me better." It breaks my heart, but that's how kids think.

Reference

Phillips, Malinda. "Walking Through the Valley of the Shadow" *The 90/Ten Project* blog, March 28, 2014, http://the90tenproject.com/2014/03/28/walking-through-the-valley-of-the-shadow.

* * *

Rebecca Hawkes was adopted as an infant and is herself an adoptive parent by way of older-child foster adoption. She has presented on adoption-related topics at various venues. Her writing has appeared at *Rebecca Hawkes, The Thriving Child, Lost Daughters, Adoption Voices Magazine, BlogHer,* and *The Huffington Post,* and in the anthologies *Lost Daughters: Writing Adoption From a Place of Empowerment and Peace* and *Adoption Reunion in the Social Media Age.* She is certified as a parenting instructor by both the Beyond Consequences Institute and Gordon Training International. She is also a trained MotherWoman facilitator and a former assistant leader for The Center for Nonviolent Communication's Parent Peer Leadership Program.

Suzanne Brita Schecker, Ed.D, LMHC has practiced psychotherapy for thirty-five years. Her work is grounded in a diverse background including training in method acting, philosophy, comparative religion, Psychosynthesis, Integrative breath work, EMDR, Compassionate Listening and mindfulness-based psychotherapy.

She offers online psychotherapy and mindfulness coaching that explores basic stillness and meditation techniques that integrate the spiritual and self-help knowledge we already have. She brings the power of mindfulness to trauma recovery, grief work, adoption, and foster care, aging, couple's and family issues and difficult life transitions. All therapy is about healing the wounds of separation from our authentic self and from those we love.

Chapter 4—The Myth of Reactive Attachment Disorder

By Jodi Haywood

The story sounds heart-wrenching when you hear it from the adoptive mother's perspective. After years of longing for a child, years of watching her name inch up the waiting list, thousands of dollars spent on legal fees and flights and everything else involved in bringing an orphaned child home from a foreign country—a child who should be overjoyed to receive all the benefits of Western culture and embrace a real home with two loving parents—the child is still unresponsive, indifferent, even hostile toward these new parents.

Things have not gone according to the plan she envisioned. Where is the laughing, playful child who responds to Mom and Dad the way their friends' and siblings' children do? Why is this one sullen and withdrawn, unwilling to make friends in play group, resistant to affection from the parents, and goes through times of switching off altogether—"spacing out" into a world that doesn't exist for anybody else? Most importantly, the bond these parents had expected to share with their child is only a one-way street.

Thoughts such as: What are we doing wrong? Parenting was never supposed to be so frustrating. The baby looked so cute in the photos on the orphanage's website. Could something be seriously wrong with her, a

mental or emotional disorder that the agency failed to
mention? After all, she should be used to us by now—it's
been over a month. Or six months. Or a year, or more.
What is the matter with her that we aren't getting
through?

The confused adoptive mother takes the child to
a psychiatrist, a presumed expert who deduces that the
child suffers from Reactive Attachment Disorder (RAD)
and outlines a course of treatment designed to help the
disconnected child form the same level of attachment
that she would have with her natural mom. After all,
that's what "as if born to" means, right?

For the adoptive caregiver, that is what it means.
The maternal instinct, combined with the belief that "this
is my child," because the papers have been signed and so
much has been invested in the adoption for so long. For
the child, though, it means confusion and turmoil. It
means she has endured being torn from her home and
thrust into the arms of strangers, an act that no words
can prepare her for and no amount of love can make up
for, not in the short term. Because this child formed the
same attachment to her own mother that every baby
does—in the womb, for the nine months when the
mother is literally the baby's entire world. Even an infant
adopted as a newborn is abruptly and inexplicably
severed from that safe world, the first and most vital
attachment of her life broken.

"But our child came from an orphanage! It wasn't
safe! The conditions were deplorable; the kids got no
attention…"

Not necessarily. The child you adopted has a past
history of which you know nothing—and speculating on
it will not alter or erase any one of the traumatic events
that marked her early life. Her mother—her natural
mother, the one she bonded with—might have kept her
for a day, a week, months, a year or more. Her mother
might have died violently or suffered repeated abuse; she
might have been coerced or tricked into surrendering her
child, or believed the separation would be temporary; the

child might have been kidnapped and sold on the black market. Prior to the separation, she must have had time to form an attachment to her mother, and no matter how impersonal the conditions were at the orphanage, she may have formed a bond with one or more caregivers there. Or she may have spent time with extended family members in interim care. It's impossible for any adoptive parent to presume to know what the child and her natural family may have endured.

My own mother fled domestic violence by taking me to live with my paternal grandparents, where she stayed with me at first, then entrusted me to their temporary care. When my grandfather died unexpectedly, my grandmother made other arrangements for me without notifying her. Only in the last year have I been able to put together most of the pieces of my own story. The point is, *nobody knows.* Adoption agencies have been known to falsify information, particularly with international adoptees, about the baby's origins and surviving relatives.

Even in my own life, growing up in a "relative adoption" with a biological aunt and her husband, I am still uncovering the secrets they kept from me and unraveling the lies they told me. I was not "given up" for adoption; my aunt took me to live with her a few months before my second birthday, then set the adoption wheels in motion. Finally, she contacted my mother to obtain her signature on the adoption documents. One of the most difficult things to believe while processing this information are the ideas that I am a worthwhile person, deserving of the truth, worthy of being loved for who I am. It's hard not to feel like a stolen family heirloom, dusted off and displayed for company while the manufacturer's stamp remains hidden from view. Do I have any value beyond that of being an exhibit in a home I didn't choose for myself?

The older the child, the more trauma she is likely to have experienced, the more separations she is likely to have endured—and the more she is likely to remember.

She may have had her parents for some time, and misses them deeply, or she may have never been truly parented—never received consistent, ongoing nurturing from at least one caregiver.

Among the criteria for a RAD diagnosis are inappropriate familiarity with strangers and multiple changes in caregivers (Schechter, et al., 2010). However, these factors alone do not automatically result in RAD.

Inappropriate familiarity with strangers

To the adoptive parent who takes the young child to a crowded shopping mall, the sight of the child suddenly breaking free from her hold and running up to a strange woman as if she's her long-lost mother is considered inappropriate behavior. There may be some jealousy involved; a child who hates to receive affection from the adoptive mother and squirms away from her attempts to cuddle, then climbs into the lap of her new Sunday school teacher during story time as if she belongs there, might be perceived as having the roles of "family" and "acquaintances" mixed up. But let's look at the situation from the child's point of view.

She might vaguely remember having a mother and being taken away from her, or her natural mother may be a physical memory rather than a cognitive one, but she knows that she has a real mother somewhere, not just this strange lady taking care of her. Consciously or not, she searches every crowd for a familiar face, scent, voice, something that might bring her mother back to her. Maybe the woman in the shopping mall has her mother's hair color, or facial features that resemble the ones she sees in her own mirror. Maybe her Sunday school teacher wears the same perfume or uses the same lotion her mother favored, and the scent makes her feel secure enough to form a bond. I remember one incident at the age of six or seven, exploring a beach with a group of kids from a summer day camp. I approached an elderly man and asked him his name. When he told me he didn't have a name, I took him seriously (unaware that he was either teasing or didn't want to tell me), and said I would call him George. My father and grandfather were both named George.

It doesn't seem to occur to people confused by this behavior that strangers are inappropriately familiar with adopted children, too. A newborn baby's close circle consists of baby and natural mother, and immediate family. The circle slowly expands as the baby becomes more aware of his or her surroundings, to include extended family and friends. When you remove a baby from this circle, place her in the arms of the couple who want to adopt her, and send her home with them, you are handing her over to strangers. When this strange woman undresses the baby and changes her diaper or bathes her, when she attempts to feed her from a bottle—after this baby has received every meal directly from her mother—although the baby cannot put it into words, she senses that this stranger is being inappropriately familiar with her.

An older child, particularly one who has already endured at least one change in caregivers prior to the adoption placement, will be even more resistant to the attempts of strangers to care for her, and more reluctant to trust. When a child has a solid relationship with the natural mother, who provides a safe "home base" to return to, appropriate boundaries can be established with additional caregivers such as daycare providers and evening babysitters. Mom will always come back. But when Mom doesn't come back, having a series of caregivers and no "home base," results in a fragmented sense of self. After a while one realizes the futility of forming an attachment to somebody who is only going to hand you off to someone else when her shift ends, or to some higher authority decides it's time for you to move on.

Multiple changes in caregivers

While the initial act of adopting, including the adoption of a newborn baby, is in effect a "rehoming" of the child, the term "rehoming" tends to be applied more frequently to the transfer of a child from one foster or adoptive home to another—from one interim caregiver or set of caregivers to another, who may or may not become a permanent part of the child's life. Either way, the child has already learned the concept of caregiver inconsistency, or parental impermanence. The fear of subsequent abandonment is in no way groundless or irrational; it is a threat constantly hanging over the child like a guillotine blade poised to sever any future attachment he or she may want to form.

"But we adopted her! It's for keeps. She has to know we're not going to abandon her like everyone else did!"

How does she "know" that? First, every parent or caregiver prior has modeled inconstancy for her. Second, she has no way of comprehending the legally binding effect of her adoption documents. Signatures on a piece of paper are not strong enough to tie her to her adoptive parents. She lacks the perspective of permanence. And third, reminding her verbally that this is "for keeps" and she is now your "forever daughter" might be more frightening than reassuring in this strange new environment. She may have a natural desire to escape, to return to the safety of the home she left, to retreat from the overwhelming closeness of strangers. You may consider her your child, but she will consider you a stranger until she herself makes the decision to place her trust in you. Until she chooses to be "on your side," you may be perceived as an enemy, a captor, holding her hostage from her own mother—even if she no longer has conscious memory of her mother.

A history of multiple caregivers—either by rehoming or living in a facility where various adults take turns caring for the child—may explain why older babies and children adopted from orphanages, particularly international adoptees, are more susceptible to a RAD diagnosis than a domestic newborn adoption. Not that earlier adoptions are free of trauma; quite the contrary. It's a different type of trauma, often with more dramatic manifestations, than that of children raised by the same adoptive caregivers from infancy.

The child from a foreign orphanage may not be able to speak yet, but he or she has certainly heard others speaking, perhaps singing. These children may not be able to introduce themselves by name, but they know their own names and respond to them. They cannot describe their surroundings with words or replicate them in drawings, but this does not make these surroundings any less familiar— any less "home" to them. It does not mean they miss home any less. And they might not know—or comprehend the meaning of—the words "mom," "dad," or "parents," but once they do, they will instinctively know that these words have no biological connection to the adults raising them. In my own case, I knew my dad. When my aunt and grandmother took me across the ocean to my "new home" at twenty-one months, I had already learned to call him Daddy. At some point, my aunt and uncle decided it was time I stopped calling them by their first names and started using parental terms for them (most likely to prepare me for the adoption home study), and it felt wrong, like I was reciting lines in a play. I must have been eleven or twelve when I went back to calling my uncle by his first name; it's how I thought of both of them. I instinctively knew I wouldn't get away with calling my aunt anything but "Mom," so I kept up that charade until her death.

Such a child subject to international adoption is not suffering from an attachment "disorder," but from Post-Traumatic Stress. There is much confusion and turmoil as he or she attempts to navigate this unsafe new reality with neither map nor guide. Everything in this environment looks different, sounds different, smells different. No face or voice is familiar. Fear and anger are

natural, instinctive responses to the "wrongness" of these
new surroundings; they are not behavioral problems in
and of themselves. The child is simply reacting normally
to abnormal and unnatural circumstances. Adoption is
not natural. International or transracial adoption is even
less natural. A grieving, traumatized child needs to remain
with known family members or other familiar caregivers
whenever possible. Thrusting them into unknown,
potentially hostile territory will only compound the
trauma. Despite being my father's sister, my adopting
aunt was a stranger to me for the first two years of my
life. She lived in another country and was no more a part
of my circle than the President of the United States. No
matter how much knowledge you have of a child prior to
taking guardianship, from letters or photographs or
contact with the orphanage, you are not part of the
child's familiar world or natural environment. That level
of belonging, of acceptance and trust, can only come with
time and patience, and every child has his or her own
time frame.

While Post-Traumatic Stress Disorder (PTSD)
takes different forms depending on its causes, Complex
(C-PTSD) or Developmental (D-PTSD) seem to be the
most logical diagnosis. "Complex," because it stems from
a series of events (abandonment or relinquishment,
followed by adoption, followed by the stress of trying to
adapt to a family other than one's own), rather than one
single traumatic event. "Developmental" because these
events take place in early childhood, sometimes beginning
with prenatal trauma, before the "self" is fully
developed—and before verbal expression and cognitive
recollection. Thus, the child lacks the reasoning capacity
to make sense of what is going on and lacks the verbal
skills to convey his or her emotions.

Much has been written recently about traumatic
memory being stored in the body, even when the
conscious mind buries it; one article I would recommend
is *The Body Keeps the Score: Memory & the Evolving
Psychobiology of Post-Traumatic Stress*, by Bessel van der

Kolk, first published in the *Harvard Review of Psychiatry* (1994).

This would explain why responses to trauma "triggers" are physical reactions, such as fight or flight— and why these reactions are instinctive rather than based on logical reasoning. It's difficult to identify a trigger when we have no conscious memory of the original traumatic event. If we don't recall being taken from our mother's arms as babies and handed over to a stranger, for example, it doesn't make "sense" to shy away from someone who reaches out to hug us when we're older. It's not "normal" to resist comfort. Yet the fear of being removed from a safe place and held against our will by a stranger has never left our body, which instinctively stiffens and refuses to feel at ease in somebody's arms. Or we may feel a heightened sense of anxiety in a room full of strangers, or a situation we are unable to control, and not understand why. Behavioral therapy will have limited success in dealing with these issues; the trauma is stored in our nervous system, and we need to rewire ourselves. Studies have shown neurological differences in people who experienced severe trauma during early childhood, such as parental abandonment or death: coping mechanisms are limited at that stage of growth, and the absence of the natural mother seems to program the brain and nervous system to believe the world is no longer a safe place (Vogel, et al., 2012).

Easing the transition by facilitating safe havens

If these reactions are indeed physical and somatic, rather than logical and cognitive, healing must take place in the same areas. The child requires a safe haven, free from stress, anxiety, and anything that triggers the unconscious memories of maternal abandonment or rejection. Since every child is unique, with his or her own history and preverbal experiences, it is up to the child to create this safe haven. The important thing to remember is: this is where the child feels safe; this is where he or she recharges emotional batteries so-to-speak. If the child shuts you out, do not take it personally. It's not up to you to determine the point at which the child becomes overwhelmed by life and needs to retreat into his or her safe zone—just as it is not up to you to decide which comforting items the child needs to surround herself with. Whenever possible, these items may come from her previous family or home, such as a doll or stuffed animal. Again, it is not up to the adoptive parent to tell the child she's too old to play with dolls, or has outgrown the teddy bear she brought from the orphanage. During times of extreme stress or anxiety, she may revert to the mental age at which she was abandoned or taken, and as long as she is clearly able to separate between past and present, memory and current reality, do not interfere. Never intrude into her safe haven, and accept the fact you may never receive an invitation. Every adopted child has a compartment of her life that does not belong to the adoptive parents.

Adoptive parents must not put the responsibility of integrating, or fitting into the family, on the child. They must not expect the child to make the necessary adjustments for a smooth transition. The child has already made all of the adjustments he or she is capable of making. She has been taken out of her element, removed from her natural environment and caregivers, suffered severe trauma. The adults who chose to adopt her are the ones who need to adjust to becoming adoptive parents. Children may be resilient in some areas, but in the instance of complex trauma, the reactions they conceal on the surface are bound to manifest themselves in other behaviors.

This child has been thrust into an environment she did not choose, where she does not feel at first that she belongs, and that sense of completely belonging may elude her for the rest of her life. One way of helping her adjust is to encourage her to make age-appropriate contributions in the decision-making processes: "Where do we want to go today? The zoo, the museum, the art gallery, or a walk along the river?" This way she doesn't feel as if she is being taken somewhere against her will (a giant trigger for adoptees), and she, along with the rest of the family, discovers her interests and favorite activities.

Do not assume the child knows how to interact properly with other children, and do not assume she doesn't. Children who have experienced a healthy, unbroken bond with their natural mother find it easier to form and maintain friendships among their own age group than those who have suffered broken attachments. He may have been the only child he's ever known; she may have had several siblings in her family of origin. Some social workers do not recommend adopting out of birth order, i.e. the oldest child in the family of origin should not become the youngest in his or her adoptive family. Regardless of whether the newly adopted child is the only one in the family or one of many, whether at home or in daycare or play group, let the child make the decisions regarding which of his or her toys may be shared with others. Yes, this does go against the child-care manuals and parental logic: the child must learn to share. But a child who has lost everyone and everything meaningful, including family and—in some cases—homeland, may be extremely reluctant to allow a favorite toy to fall into the hands of a potentially hostile stranger. Certain items, within reason, should remain the exclusive territory of the adopted child until he or she opens up enough to share them.

Other areas of the adopted child's safe haven may include activities such as an athletic or creative outlet. Do not force the child to participate in activities just because you have always wanted a baseball player or a ballerina; allow him or her to try new things, observe the child without smothering or manipulating, and let he or she develop personal interests. Creative expression such as art or writing can be very beneficial to the child, but allow some privacy; let the child show you a drawing and explain what it means, but don't flip through the drawing pad on your own, and never read the child's journal. Again, this is a trust issue. Everybody, parent or child, natural or adopted, has their own set of personal boundaries. These boundaries get blurred in adopted children as parents become strangers and strangers attempt to take the place of parents. For me, my writing was a very private thing, as my own room was a very private space, and I kept the door closed at all times to shut out my aunt and uncle. They had intruded enough in my life, and I needed safe zones where I could strip off my costume, peel off the mask, and drop the charade for a short time in order to breathe. If I ever caught my aunt reading one of the stories I'd written or my uncle leafing through the drawings in my desk drawers, I felt as if I had been physically violated. Sometimes it was easier to keep the words inside, go for a long run and sweat it out.

Pets are a wonderful companion on the healing journey; a dog, especially, may become an unofficial therapy animal simply by bonding with the child. Animals are sensitive and intuitive, offer unconditional love and affection, and allow a child to focus on the needs of another without the uncertainty of what may be expected in return. Take the child to an animal shelter and allow him or her to choose a new best friend. Allow them to bond and grow accustomed to one another. One important thing to remember is, while there may be parallels between adopting your child and adopting a shelter animal, don't compare the two aloud. Leave it to the child to make the connection. The child is a human being, not a dog or a cat, and will gradually establish his or her own independence. Bringing a pet into the home will also help the child understand his or her place in the family. Some adoptive parents, while telling the child's narrative, may use certain words that sound positive to their own ears but don't inspire such warm and fuzzy feelings in the child, particularly an older child who feels capable of telling his or her own story. It is very important for any child, but especially adoptees, to "own their narrative" and tell the adoption story from their own point of view.

One of the most important things to remember is that no child, natural or adopted, is a possession. Each of us is an individual person with our own history, needs, dreams and fears, likes and dislikes. Every one of us requires the freedom to choose who is allowed in our circle of trust and who is not. Signing a set of papers to adopt a child does not automatically give you the key to their inner sanctuary. If they choose to withhold that key from you, or to place it in somebody else's hands, do not punish them for that choice.

My viewpoint, both personal and professional, is that parents are not replaceable. Regardless of their circumstances, relinquished, orphaned, or otherwise, children are in need of caregivers, not new parents. Just as adopting a child cannot erase the loss of a stillborn or miscarried biological baby; your presence in the child's life is not a magic wand that causes traumatic events or their effects to vanish. Attachment issues and bonding difficulties are not illnesses that can be cured; they are the result of deep hurts that must be treated with love, patience and tenderness. These wounds must be allowed to heal over time, and the scars from these wounds must be accepted as part of the whole child, as you would accept a physical or mental limitation. Rather than broken people in need of fixing, we need to be treated as whole people with strengths and shortcomings.

References

Schechter, Daniel S. and Erica Willheim. "Disturbances of Attachment and Parental Psychopathology in Early Childhood" in *Child and Adolescent Psychiatric Clinics of North America*, 18 (3): 665-686. DOI: 10.1016/j.chc.2009.03.001.

Vogel, Sarah and Maggie Brown. "Childhood trauma and its neurological legacy," in *Paediatrics*, September 12, 2012, http://www.ausmed.com.au/blog/entry/childhood-trauma-and-its-neurological-legacy.

* * *

Jodi Haywood is an adoptee in reunion, a wife, mom, stepmom, writer, and marathon runner. Taken from her native Britain at age two, she grew up in a closed relative adoption which, while psychologically damaging, greatly influenced her storytelling abilities. Her writing credits include two "slightly twisted" young adult novels (and many more in the works), a church history book, contributions to adoption anthologies, and her memoir/case study work-in-progress, *Attachment Unavailable*, which has its own Facebook page. She recently returned to college to complete a psychology degree, with the goal toward a career in post-adoption/developmental trauma therapy.

Chapter 5— Heeding the Body's Messages: Body–Mind Implications of Prenatal Trauma

By Marcy Axness, Ph.D. and Raja Selvam, Ph.D.

*T*he year was 1995 and I was just concluding an eighteen-month bout of primal therapy. (I say "bout," because going back to therapy always felt to me a bit like coming down with something... again.) I was thirty-nine-years-old, and reeling from the relational demands of motherhood. Though my children Ian and Eve were eight and four, I was struggling to navigate the inner upheaval that came with their births. Looking back now it's so clear: as an adopted person whose birth mother emotionally detached from me during pregnancy... who had been separated from her at birth... and then not parented with much affection or attention... I learned at a basic, primal level that it was natural, normal, and safe to be alone. To be disconnected. I was the classic hyper-achieving, always-gleaming good adoptee with higher-than-average (pseudo) self-esteem.

Then Ian had come along. Mothering broke me open. My stolid fortresses of defense and control, my "Things are perfect, I'm handling everything fine" persona that had thwarted a few earnest attempts at therapy over the years finally began to shred under the pumice of my son's raw, baby neediness, his control-shattering toddler defiance, and the terrifying demands of intimacy that children innocently exact. Three years later, on the day before Eve was born, I experienced a spontaneous prenatal regression: an eruption of

*ancient tears accompanied by the words coming out of my mouth,
"Mommy doesn't want me... Mommy doesn't want me."*

*I reconnected with Annette Baran (whom I had
interviewed twelve years prior for a CBS program on adoptees). I
asked her about this "crazy" notion I had: "Is it possible that
adoptees come into the world already wounded?" Annette told me
about Nancy Verrier, who was writing about something called "the
primal wound." (This was 1993 and* The Primal Wound
*wouldn't be published for a year yet.) My antennae went up. I knew
I was on to something. I was then led to learning about prenatal
psychology, which in turn led me to primal therapy. Returning to my
womb-life and my birth was cathartic and enlightening, and was
certainly an important piece of my puzzle at the time. But just as we
were nearing the end of our work together, I began to have bodily
expressions that my therapist was untrained to interpret or help me
resolve. For example, my legs would start shaking uncontrollably. I
was also attending a triad support group around this time, and I
would have the same shaking-leg thing happen in the circle as we
discussed our various stories and issues.*

*As synchronicity would have it, right around this time I
saw an article on childhood trauma by Peter Levine in* Mothering
*magazine. It spoke directly to some of the symptoms I was having,
as well as certain features of my lifelong experience. I wrote Dr.
Levine a letter (a snail-mail letter, how quaint!) and he responded
with the suggestion I contact Raja Selvam, one of his top students
who happened to live and work in my Southern California area. I
called Dr. Selvam and in just ten minutes on the phone, he captured
my lived experience with such uncanny specificity and accuracy that I
made an appointment with him on the spot.*

*The following interview took place sometime during my
year of transformative work with Raja, and unfolds from the
premise, well-established in pre- and perinatal research, that very
early circumstances matter in deep and lasting ways. To be conceived
without being intended, to be carried in the womb of a stressed
mother facing a crisis pregnancy, leave lifelong traces that usually
persist without an understanding of their origins. More can be found
in my opening chapter (co-authored with Joel Evans) in the new
book,* Women's Reproductive Mental Health Across the
Lifespan, *entitled "Pre- and Perinatal Influences on Female*

Mental Health" (many pages are available to read on Amazon), or in the short blog post, "Mental Health Begins in the Womb" (Axness, 2013).

I imagine this is a new, and possibly dismaying, concept to many— that rejection and abandonment issues so common to adoptees can begin as early as this. Some folks are still wrapping their minds around the idea that they can begin with postpartum separation, which Nancy Verrier elucidated in her classic book, The Primal Wound, *and I summarize in a blog post called, "The Wound of Mother-Newborn Separation" (Axness, 2014). While some of the somatic and nervous system implications overlap, in this interview we zero-in on the lesser-explored embodied imprints of prenatal stress/trauma.*

Marcy Axness—If you had just a few minutes with an adoptee, or anyone who has suffered severe stress in the womb …

Raja Selvam—… what would I tell them? Well, on the emotional level, it's very reasonable that they would feel not wanted, that they didn't belong. On the physical level, people who have had this kind of trauma will have symptoms like—we're talking about how it would affect the physiology in their life later—a lot of problems around the stomach. They often will have curvature of the spine, they may have eye problems. These are all physical symptoms, and what they really are is the body's early attempt to deal with high, high levels of excitation that they cannot discharge, which is the trauma. We categorize prenatal trauma as global shock trauma, which is the most severe in its impact.

Here's what happens in the womb: The child is very visceral. It has more of the sympathetic, or excitation, branch of the autonomic nervous system and less of the parasympathetic, or calming, branch in place. It depends on its mother's system, and when it senses that it's not wanted, it's distressed. It's extremely distressed, with no end in sight. The level of physical excitation is so much that they can't handle it, that it's almost like they're going to fragment into a thousand pieces if they're allowed to have it, so the reptilian brain, which has the wisdom of billions of years of evolution, is going to do something about it, right? So what it's going to do is disorganize itself; tighten the stomach, for example, twist away from the uterine wall, because at some level, the wall of the uterus itself becomes an enemy, if you think about it. There's no warmth there. So they sort of twist away from it. Often the breathing function gets affected, so the child breathes little. Then it doesn't have to feel, doesn't have to sense the energy.

Marcy—Yes, I've had this sense for so long, about not breathing deeply.

Raja—And it will tighten the umbilical cord area, the viscera, enough to cut off from the mother's rejecting energy, or whatever energy or substance that the child doesn't want—if the mother is drinking, any number of things. It's like, "Can I cut myself off from the mother who's distressing me?" Unfortunately, no, because the child's completely in the mother's energy system, totally dependent on it, but it's going to try to.

Marcy—So that constriction in various central parts of the fetus is an attempt to …

Raja—It is an attempt to hold back this tremendous excitation and escalation that threatens to fragment the autonomic nervous system and to threaten its very survival.

Marcy—This sensing by the fetus that it's not wanted—is it primarily a telepathic communication?

Raja—No, I'm talking about physical.

Marcy—Chemical?

Raja—It's biochemical, but it's also the tissue. For example, if a mother does not want the child, the walls of the uterus will not be friendly for the child.

Marcy—In what way?

Raja—Sensate loss. For example, if I work with a client who does not have energy in the legs, the legs are really cold. What do we do when we want to forget pain in a certain part of the body, or we don't want to feel certain parts of the body? Sometimes women who have shame about their breasts will draw energy from the breasts—they won't even feel them. In that way, the mother will try to avoid even feeling, and the child senses it—the communication is totally in the sensate realm. And remember that the mother and the baby are one at that stage, so as the baby is trying to get away from its mother, it's really trying to get away from itself. Can you imagine the existential dilemma of it? So the only way it can survive is by going deeper into its core.

Have you heard of the schizoid structure, in bioenergetics? In Bodynamics—that's a body psychotherapy system that was developed by Lisbeth Marcher in Denmark—it's also called the mental existence structure. The vacant look, the "nobody home" look: there's absolutely no energy in the body, and they will be extremely intellectual. Very much in the head. That's because it had to be incredibly painful for the fetus to be otherwise. When the child is not wanted at all, it will be very hard for them to be in their feelings as they grow up.

But if they feel wanted, and then something suddenly happens during the pregnancy—the mother has a difficult experience, or severe stress—then they go into a defense of a very emotional nature. That's a different survival strategy, what is called—in Bodynamics—the emotional existence structure. Often they will have a lot of energy. Janis Joplin is a classic example of emotional existence structure.

Marcy—Do you think the fetus differentiates between types of negative energy, between direct rejection by the mother and, say, more general acute stress in the mother, or her negative feelings toward someone other than the baby? Was this sped-up autonomic nervous system response I experienced in my mother's womb in response to just her stress directly, or was it me, on some level, as a fetus, knowing—or interpreting—that my mother had rejected me?

Raja—Cognitive?

Marcy—Not cognitive, but maybe on some telepathic level, or more on a spiritual level—it's essentially spiritual, I believe.

Raja—The fetus doesn't know, I'll give you an example. A loving mother, she was painting the baby's room. The fumes from the paint were poisonous. The mother did not know it, and she was inhaling it, and the baby was getting slowly poisoned. Out of which came this notion that it was an attack on her life, and that translated into her feeling of her mother not wanting her. This child grew up with the emotional existence structure. She's very emotional, she was fully in her feelings a lot, and she always had the feeling that the world, and people in it, the animals in it, would disappear from her life any time. And this was the child of a mother who really wanted her. So fetuses are capable of misunderstanding what's going on.

Marcy—Misinterpreting.

Raja—Yes, exactly. So on some level, stress is stress. But the thing is that it affects the physiology. The meaning is born of the distress in the physiology. It's all happening in the realm of sensation. In the fetus, the emotional, cognitive capabilities are not as developed as the sensate capabilities, so it's all happening in the realm of the primitive brain. And so it will twist away from the wall of the uterus, and that's where scoliosis might come from, and it has a purpose. When we can twist our spinal column in that way, we can often block the energy, the energy in the body, so the excitation can be blocked.

Marcy—So that is the reason—the blocking of the energy? About stopping what it is that's hurting, which is this over-excitation, over-flow of energy?

Raja—Over-excitation is actually close to death, it's like putting your finger into the electric socket.

Marcy—So the constriction, as a protective response to the over-excitation, is like jamming a stick into the gears? It makes everything shut down, but at least it shuts down the threat?

Raja—But the energy is bound in the gears that have been stopped. So to follow with your analogy, you're looking at somebody running at, let's say, eighty miles per hour and then stopping suddenly. If you stop a machine going at the rate of eighty mph all of a sudden, then the potential energy is still stuck in the machine. So when we take the stick out, there's an amazing amount of energy. You have to take it out slowly; if you take it out quickly, it's going to throw another stick into itself—in fact, the excitation will be at a higher level. Because at least the initial build-up was gradual. But now if you're going to take the stick out and all of that excitation is going to be allowed to flow, it actually will be a higher level of energy. So we take the stick out very slowly. And you take that released energy, we take that into the person's life, and see how they can use it.

Marcy—Right, because that's the flip side: I've been chronically low-energy all of my life, and I've always had this sort of idea that the low energy, the blocking of the energy, had to do with the idea that if I block the energy from flowing, then I block whatever the real feelings are that are underneath it all. I mean, if my energy is going to start flowing, if the juices are going to start flowing, I'll start feeling what I'm trying not to feel all my life.[1] Is that right?

---

[1] My own experience as an adoptee was described so well by Alice Miller. In her clinical research of people who, due to very early trauma, sustained damage to their core sense of self, she found that they "are children who have not been free to experience the very earliest feelings, such as discontent, anger, rage, pain, even hunger and, of course, enjoyment of their bodies" (Miller, 1981).

Integrative Body Psychotherapy practitioners Jack Rosenberg and Marjorie Rand, extending the body-based therapeutic traditions of Reich and Lowen (Lowen, et al., 1975), point out the central role played by the denial of the body in the genesis of defensive personality styles. "The baby whose needs aren't taken care of and who seals off his feelings, is forming blocks to his energy flow. Since all his reactions are in his body, the blocks are his growing muscular tension. ... In blocking off feelings, he stifles the flow of energy, and the core of his being—his sense of Self—lies hidden within" (Rosenberg, et al., 1985). Lowen explains how such an adult rationalizes the split.

> The sense of self depends on the perception of what goes on in the living body. One can only discard the actual self-image by denying the reality of an *embodied* self. Narcissists don't deny that they have bodies. Their grasp on reality is not that weak. But they see the body as an instrument of the mind, subject to their will. It operates only according to their images, without feeling. Although the body can function efficiently as an instrument, perform like a machine, or impress one as a statue, it then lacks "life." And it is this feeling of aliveness that gives rise to the experience of the self.
>
> We can speak of a false self-set up against the true self, but I prefer to describe the split in terms of an image that contradicts the self, and to see the basic disturbance as a conflict between the image and the bodily self. ... One can only [deny one's feelings] by dissociating the ego from the body, the foundation of one's aliveness. And one has to keep up a constant effort to suppress all feeling, to act "as if" (Lowen, 1975).

There is agreement on the fact that such "constant effort to suppress" not only creates defensive muscular blockages (what Reich and Lowen term "armoring"), it also puts a constant drain on organismic energy, often leading to chronic illness and fatigue. This lack of aliveness due to suppressed feelings and blocked energy, together with the self/image split and the acting "as if," had characterized my lifelong experience.

Raja—Yes, absolutely. And the point is, traumas this early in life very often get lodged in the physiology.

Marcy—And that's the whole point of this kind of work. That's the whole point of my having gone through all this emotional work for years, and finding that I still have this revving in my stomach. I've done a lot of cathartic work.

Raja—And it helped, I'm sure. The emotional work is extremely important to bring about connection to the rest of the world, but at the same time, to be fully in the body, to experience the pleasure of daily life, to have the energy available, it's important to do the physiological work. The extra advantage is the following: sensations often provide the container for the emotions, so often when people are able to resolve the physiology, they're able to then contain more of their emotions, and somehow feel more fulfilled in their life. Because ultimately, life is about how you feel about your children, your spouse, your life every day.

Marcy—Right, that's why I've experienced so much relief with the work I've done. But it's why I'm left with this residue of physical responses.

Raja—The effects of early over-stimulation. It's really over-stimulation that the equipment couldn't handle, that's what trauma is to a fetus, because it has no cognition as to what has happened. It only senses massive over-stimulation. So that's going to permeate everything, it's under everything, any issue that is there in the client's life. Another symptom of early trauma is that any time any kind of excitation starts to happen, good or bad, it will tap into the anxiety.

Marcy—Right. Say a little bit more about that.

Raja—Anytime you have a good thing happen to you, what does that mean? Excitation. Anytime you have something bad happen to you, what does that mean? Excitation. It will immediately tap into that prenatal anxiety. It's almost like any other issue finds a trap door, a shortcut to this kind of state. It permeates everything, it really permeates everything. It's what people generally describe as "feeling anxious." But it isn't about present-day. It's really the anxiety of death. It's really not emotional anxiety, but survival anxiety of the reptilian core. And that does not come from a thought in the new brain, it comes from this very early experience, and that's why it often doesn't make sense, you know what I mean?

Marcy—Absolutely. You can't put your finger on it. That reminds me of the issue we once spoke about—the experience of not being able to focus, to concentrate on one task. When I get into that revved-up state, I'm often also very scattered in that way, bouncing from one thing to another.

Raja—It's called the *orienting response gone awry*. A typical orienting response for an animal in the wild will be what? It hears a noise and it crouches, tightens the stomach, goes down on its haunches, turns around and looks. There's a good deal of excitement, of physical arousal. And then it sees that it's just a feather or something, and so it just releases, and goes on its way. That's the classic orienting response, and we need that in order to deal with danger.

When we have traumatized physiology, it means that there is arousal—when we talked about this, you'd experienced the arousal after hearing your birth mother's voice on the phone—and what happens is because there's arousal, the reptilian brain looks around—"Where's the danger, where's the danger?" You cannot focus on any one thing, because you quickly realize that the danger isn't there. So you unfocus on that thing and refocus on another, but soon the anxiety rises again. Because there is really no danger *outside of you*. The "danger" is an internal sensation. So that's why it gave you relief to go from one activity to the next, but as soon as you start to focus on one, there is again increased arousal because at some level you see that that book, or project—whatever you were trying to focus on—was not the danger, it must be elsewhere. So the reptilian brain keeps trying to make you figure out where the danger is.[2]

So it has to do with the ability of the autonomic nervous system to be flexible enough to handle varying levels of energy or excitation. We have to calibrate it, so to speak, over time. It's almost like, you have a body, and it can handle, let's say, five watts of energy at a time, but its potential is something like eighty watts or ninety watts. And I cannot go from five watts to eighty watts in one day.

Marcy—But that's what doing catharsis is.

Raja—Yes, catharsis, what it could do—does— although it may be resolving other things at other levels, emotionally—it could release so much wattage into the system, that physiologically the system might get re-traumatized. And one thing that I noticed when I worked with you: you were in a state of arousal, so it was very easy to work with that, as opposed to when it actually becomes symptoms.

For example, if you come to me with some tension in your shoulder that is really bad, that would have been a symptom that the arousal had been split off and stored in a certain part of the body to manage the excess activation. And that is what spinal curvature is about, and most fetuses that have fetal distress develop some degree of that. What they're really trying to do is to somewhat store that energy someplace around the spine.

---

[2] I happen to think that this could be key to a better understanding of attention-deficit disorders in adoptees and others who have experienced early loss or trauma!

And as the scoliosis straightens, energy is released into the system. But if they went and got deep-tissue work on the scoliosis, it would release so much energy so fast that the body would get re-traumatized again, and the scoliosis would come back. So that's why it's important to release a little at a time.

Marcy—One therapist I spoke with feels that people may need to have some catharsis in the beginning—and she used the analogy of an oil well—to release that initial pressure, so you can then get in there and create that energy flow so that you can channel and utilize it.

Raja—That might be the case, but it can be done in different ways and in a different order. It depends on the person. It's not that the cathartic model is a bad model, I think all those conclusions clients made early in life have to be addressed emotionally, such as "I'm not wanted" or "I don't have a right to live," things like that. And catharsis really comes from that realm. It's just that intense breathwork has to be avoided when it is contra-indicated by the presence of an unstable nervous system. It is pumping a lot of energy into the nervous system, and here's a system that cannot handle it. So in the catharsis, it could actually get re-traumatized. And the worst thing is that people actually get addicted to the catharsis; there are biochemicals secreted during catharsis, so that's another problem. For example, holotropic breathwork[3] might be a bad idea in some respect when there is severe early trauma with shock involved, even though it might

---

[3] Holotropic Breathwork™ is an experiential therapeutic practice that utilizes intensified breathing (hyperventilation) to facilitate the "non-specific amplification of a person's psychic process," which can often include emotional catharsis of previously suppressed or unrecognized feelings. Though directed intensified breathing (breathwork) has been used in many various therapies going back to the 1940's and probably before, Stanislov Grof's term "Holotropic Breathwork" is often (mistakenly) used to describe breathwork in general.

also give the person a connection to their early past for the first time—access to feelings they had not been able to get to prior.

Marcy—Like what they do in rebirthing[4], and things like that?

Raja—Right. Which is not necessarily bad. It works for some people, and it doesn't work for some people. We need to also monitor what is happening to their survival physiology, is it getting worse or better? I have run into a number of people who have developed severe symptoms like autoimmune disorders and chronic fatigue after engaging in prolonged cathartic work with early trauma.

Marcy—In talking to a few therapists about rebirthing, it seems like it can be a very unintegrated experience. You take someone, not knowing what their history is, or their past experience with any healing work, and you charge them up with all the breathing, and they can just go into all sorts of intense experiences, and ...

Raja—... can get very fragmented. Yes, what might happen there is that people dissociate. They go into the transpersonal realm, they go into altered states, like their astral body, and start seeing archetypes. And that is really not the human level. It is not necessarily bad, and

---

[4] Rebirthing is a therapeutic technique developed in the 1970s by Leonard Orr, involving intensified breathing to facilitate the re-experiencing of memories (particularly prenatal and birth, hence the name) and to release feelings and behavioral patterns associated/bound up with those memories. Particularly in a volume specific to adoption, it needs to be explicitly clarified that Orr's rebirthing is not the same as the variant "rebirthing therapy" aimed at stimulating the birth process to treat children with Reactive Attachment Disorder. This variation gained public attention in 2000 following the death by asphyxiation of ten-year-old Candace Newmaker as a result of such a session.

for some people they have such larger experiences of themselves for the first time, and that is good as long as it is not a habitual place they go to in order to defend against being also human. But again we need to monitor whether they are getting re-traumatized on a very basis level of the body and brain and experiencing traumatic stress in the process.

Marcy—That "not human" level, where we're dissociated from our most basic in-the-flesh experience— that's where a lot of us have lived all our lives.

Raja—The harder thing to do is to be—

Marcy— ... in your body.

Raja—Yes. That's where the pleasure is. The idea is to really allow the person to have as much energy as possible in the body, so that they can have as much pleasure as life is capable of giving. And charging the system with as much energy as possible and as much emotion as possible might be indicated when there is enough capacity in the nervous system, enough stability in the physiology, to handle that so that it can organize itself into even a more complex container for good as well as bad experiences that are part and parcel of human life.

Marcy—Right, and that is my lifetime experience, of not being able to have enough energy. There are times when I think of all the things I would do—especially with my kids—if I had more energy. Isn't that ultimately what the defense was against?

Raja—Exactly.

Marcy—So let's say you've got someone who comes to you who's done some work on later developmental stages in their life, but hasn't addressed any deeper or earlier, foundational trauma.[5] I would imagine that had I come in here at that stage—even as recently as three or four years ago—and started doing the kind of quiet, reflective, inward-looking work you do, I would've just started crying, like the oil well that needs to have the pressure bled off.

Raja—What would I do in that case? I would absolutely follow that, but I would monitor you to make sure that your physiology is not getting traumatized at the same time. Birth trauma is a physical trauma as well, and

---

[5] I'll use myself as an example: I went to my first therapist at age twenty-one, due to having "intimacy issues" with my boyfriend. My therapist's notes after my first session and a battery of psychological tests included the following:

> *Marcy's main personality problem is in the area of trust, intimacy, and control. Her whole personality is organized around over-determined needs for independence, self-reliance and invulnerability to others. She has strong needs to be in control behaviorally and emotionally, and she is competitive with very strong achievement needs. Her over-determined need for independence appears from the tests to be dynamically related to strong, unmet dependency needs. She tries to be strong, independent and in control, and the test suggests that this is based on the strong defense against early frustration at not having her infantile child dependency needs satisfied.*

One of the first things this therapist said to me was, "It's as if you sat alone in your crib, looked around, and realized 'I've got to take care of myself, because no one else around here is going to'…" The fact is, this is probably quite right and it was a big revelation to me at the time, initiating an important and helpful reframing of much of my life. But many of the underlying issues—the mistrust that is at the heart of "intimacy issues," the core self-structure fissures—weren't ultimately changed much, because I had in fact felt all alone, on my own, and traumatized long before I sat in my crib. The concept of a newborn as a blank slate—John Locke's *tabula rasa*—persists so strongly in our culture (despite considerable research refuting it) that even the idea of newborn separation as trauma is virtually unrecognized within the psychotherapy field, let alone prenatal trauma. And even though it was still just the dawn of pre- and perinatal psychology at the time, I still find it unfathomable that in my year of work with this therapist, the topic of my adoption *was NEVER mentioned!*

that has to be dealt with, and if that isn't dealt with, people can actually go into more and more shock as they go into more and more catharsis. So just having that in one's consciousness is good, because—

Marcy—That will allow you to notice if all of a sudden you're feeling numb or speedy, or disconnected, whatever.

Raja—Exactly. See, the idea is to really keep you here in the present. Take an issue that you're dealing with—noise, children, whatever—and then use that to open up the energy a little more. It goes through a cycle, and very often I'm just waiting for the physical body to kick in, the self-regulation to kick in.

Marcy—Tell me about the self-regulation. It's something very heartening to me to know that it isn't all just me having to do it with my mind, that there is an actual physiological process going on.

Raja—You're looking at the reptilian brain, which governs all the autonomic processes, which really has billions of years of stored wisdom. And it regulates the heartbeat—slows it down, speeds it up, etc.—it does all these things with no conscious input. It is that system that goes awry in trauma. Self-regulation is somehow thwarted. And it is not able to come back into homeostasis, because what happens is, in trauma, the autonomic nervous system is pumped up with a high level of energy, which is the reason for the stress, and it somewhat disorganizes itself to protect itself, but it's not able to go back to the normal state.

So all that we do here is that we try to bring the self-regulation back over a period of time, so that it's on its way. We give it support, with some understanding, some knowledge of how to do it, how slowly to do it, what to watch for, so on and so forth.

Marcy—But it does learn, the nervous system can still re-learn?

Raja—Yes, of course. Now the new brain can come in and spoil it as much it can help heal it. For instance, I had a client, and I didn't know that she was doing chanting.[6] She was getting better, and then she would come back and say that she was getting worse. I didn't know what happened, and then I found out she was chanting four hours a day, and really pumping so much energy into this nervous system, when it was [supposed to be] healing. So you can interfere with it by wanting to do too much.

Marcy—If someone wants to address these issues, but doesn't have the opportunity to work with someone who's familiar with it, is there anything that can be done on one's own?

Raja—Take time out, and if you have a garden nearby, some place that you like, go there. See, one way to bring back the self-regulation is to go to nature.

Marcy—That's something that I've always heard, and yet I have always had this disinclination to go out into nature, even though I know it's supposed to be healing.

Raja—You see, in trauma all connection is broken. The connection to nature is broken, the connection to the healing resources is broken. And we try to reestablish that. Ida Rolf said once, "If you did not get it from your mother, get it from *the* Mother, the earth." That connection is broken, so it's not surprising that there is some resistance there.

---

[6] Reciting specific words, phrases or tones in a rhythmic, repetitive way—usually associated with a particular spiritual practice—can generate significant energy within the system, similar to breathwork.

Marcy—Yeah, it's like I want to just stay in the house, and look at the trees from inside.

Raja—That's fine, to start with, to connect with it from there. You see, nature's rhythm is so strong, that it can really influence us when we start to vibrate with it. You know when people who are really hyper go to the ocean and conk out? Because the natural rhythm of the ocean is overwhelming, so their mechanism that is resisting self-regulation gets pulled into the natural rhythm and it starts to regulate itself.

Marcy—When we were doing this work one day, I was a little surprised to get these very vivid, rather dramatic [snakes in my stomach, chest filled with wet clay] images, when I don't consider myself to have a particularly vivid or soaring visual imagination.

Raja—You're working in a very subconscious dream space. It's very non-linear, like snakes and mud. In dream space there's no time logic and no space logic. And in this healing, on the reptilian level, there's no logic. It's a place of infinite creativity, but it's *your* creativity. In trauma, it is this connection to the creativity that is broken, and which we seek to restore. This work is really about empowering the client, re-connecting them with their creative—and physiological—resources.

References

Axness, Marcy. "Mental Health Begins in the Womb" *Marcy Axness, PhD* blog, January 7, 2013, http://marcyaxness.com/parenting-for-peace/mental-health-begins-in-the-womb/.

Axness, Marcy and Joel Evans. "Pre- and Perinatal Influences on Female Mental Health," in *Women's*

Reproductive Mental Health Across the Lifespan. Edited by Diana Lynn Barnes. New York: Springer, 2014.

Axness, Marcy. "The Wound of Mother-Newborn Separation" *Mothering* blog, January 24, 2014, http://www.mothering.com/articles/the-wound-of-mother-newborn-separation/.

Lowen, Alexander. *Bioenergetics.* New York: Penguin Books, 1975.

Miller, Alice. *The Drama of the Gifted Child.* New York: Basic Books, 1981.

Rosenberg, Jack , Marjorie Rand, and Diane Asay. *Body, Self and Soul: Sustaining Integration.* Atlanta, GA: Humanics Limited, 1985.

* * *

Marcy Axness, Ph.D., author of *Parenting for Peace: Raising the Next Generation of Peacemakers*, is a leading authority in the fields of early human development, adoption, prenatal psychology, and interpersonal neurobiology. Using as a narrative foundation her experiences as an adoptee and a mother, she writes and speaks internationally on parenting, society, and the needs of children. One of the world's few experts in the primal issues involved in adoption, Dr. Axness has taught prenatal development at the graduate level and has a private practice coaching parents and "pre-parents" around the world. She is the mother of two peacemakers, Ian and Eve, both in their twenties. She invites you to join her at www.MarcyAxness.com.

Raja Selvam, Ph.D. is a senior trainer in Peter Levine's Somatic Experiencing (SE) professional trauma training programs, and the developer of the Integral

Somatic Psychotherapy (ISP) approach. His background includes body-oriented psychotherapy systems of Somatic Experiencing and Bodynamic Analysis, Jungian and archetypal psychologies, and the Intersubjective and Object Relations schools of psychoanalysis. His larger understanding of the psyche is informed by his background in Advaita Vedanta, a spiritual tradition from India. He teaches extensively in Asia, Europe, South America, Canada, and the U.S.

Chapter 6—Creating Closeness and Creating Distance: What Therapists Need to Know To Help Adoptees Increase Their Capacity for Emotional Connection

By Karen Caffrey, LPC, JD

Home is the place where, when you have to go there, they have to take you in...
—Robert Frost, *Death of a Hired Man*

The capacity for emotional closeness in relationships is at the core of psychological and spiritual well-being. Feelings of safety, trust, and belonging in our most intimate relationships—the feeling of "home"—is what gives both children and adults the ability to walk out the door in the morning, face challenges, grow, and learn.

Unsatisfying relationships, often characterized by lack of closeness, are at least part of what ails almost everyone who walks into my office. The reasons are as varied as flakes of snow. However, adoptees have an underlying similarity of experience that frequently contributes to their difficulty establishing the closeness they desire. Every adoptee has experienced a grievous loss of her first and arguably most intimate relationship: the relationship with the woman within whose body she resided for her first nine months of life. That is where we all develop our first sense of home.

In addition, most adoptees have been on the receiving end of a multitude of inappropriate responses to this initial loss (and its inevitable related losses) by their families and society, including but not limited to denial, avoidance, and shaming. To further complicate matters, most adoptees do not have a conscious, verbal memory of the initial loss, or an understanding of how it may be impacting them later on in life.

In approaching this topic, I imagine a therapist-colleague asking for advice about counseling their client who is adopted, and particularly one who has issues about creating and maintaining closeness in their relationships. What do I think would be helpful for this therapist to know about being adopted in order for him or her to best help a client?

What therapists need to know, and why

For many years the dominant cultural narrative in America has actively denied the distinctiveness of being adopted. My sad experience in speaking with adoptees who have come to me after receiving counseling from other therapists is that far too often, these counselors (who may be excellently qualified in other respects) lack the education, training, and basic knowledge about the experience of being adopted to adequately help their adoptee clients. Worse, I've seen some adoptees whose therapists actively dismissed or denied the impact of being adopted on their client's lives and concerns. This is as damaging to an adoptee as it would be to tell a person of color that race is not a factor in her life, or in how she experiences herself as being subject to discrimination. In my opinion, counseling adoptees requires a specific competency about the experience of being adopted, both intra-psychically and within our culture.

Of course the simple fact of being adopted does not mean that every adoptee needs therapy, any more than it means every member of any other minority group needs therapy. It does mean that if your client is the member of a minority group like adoptees, you need to be aware of the unique experience of that group.

The beginning: Piercing the myth of beneficial secrecy

Most adoptees who enter your office will have been raised in a "closed" (secret) or partially closed adoption, meaning that they were raised without information about their origins. Many people are surprised to learn that secrecy in adoption is a historically aberrant practice. Secrecy in adoption was a social experiment that lasted for about fifty years from the mid-to-late 1900s, and that is now recognized as contrary to the best interests of all involved.

In the early 1900s children born out of wedlock ("bastards") were considered to carry "bad blood" they inherited from their "immoral" mothers. They were placed in orphanages, on orphan trains, or farmed out in apprenticeships to people who knew their identities. In that era, the idea of hiding a child's origins from the public was actually a compassionate, socially progressive response to protect a child from this "stigma of illegitimacy." It was also a tactic used to convince prospective adoptive parents that a child was *tabula rasa,* who could be rescued from the immoral taint of the child's origins by a proper upbringing. In the mid-1900s secrecy was expanded to hide the identity of a mother from the child and adoptive parents, as well as the public, in an attempt to protect her from the shame of (having been caught) having sexual relations outside of marriage.

Given these historical antecedents, it is easy to see how the myth developed that secrecy about one's origins was beneficial to adoptees. Adoptees who questioned this secrecy were considered ungrateful (for having been rescued from their unsavory origins by the savior adoptive parents), potentially dangerous (for threatening the whitewashed, re-made virginal status of their birth mother), and psychologically suspect themselves (perhaps because their bad blood was showing).

I doubt there is a therapist alive who believes that secrecy (viz.—hiding information that is relevant to a person about themselves) is a solid basis for mental health. Yet this is the life circumstance in which most adoptees have been raised. It can be very difficult for the non-adopted to imagine what it is like to have essential, basic facts about one's identity withheld from oneself by both family members and society at large. It takes an active effort on the part of therapists to become aware of their own conscious or unconscious participation in this cultural myth and pierce their collusion in it.

Beyond the myth: The reality of the adoptee's initial loss

The reality is that all adoptees have experienced the loss of their first and most intimate biological relationship with the woman whose body they inhabited for the first nine months of life. This is a profound somatic, pre-verbal and pre-cognitive loss.

From that loss onward, every adoptee will have a different history. Some will have been placed as infants in foster care for a matter of days, months or years while some may be placed in their adoptive families immediately or while relatively young. Some may have had several foster care placements/primary caregiver changes, all of which are critical to the adoptee's narrative. The common experience is premature breaking of an intense, biological and emotional attachment to their mother.

Our species has evolved to require a long, intensive period of nurture of the young by our biological mother and extended families. There is an ever-increasing body of scientific literature that supports the profound influence of early life experience on our psychological lives. These range from studies which show that infants recognize their mother's smell, to new brain imaging techniques that are offering objective insights into the subjective experience of attachment, intimacy, and relationship. Separating an infant from her biological mother would, from an evolutionary perspective, most likely result in death.

Successful therapists practice from a myriad of theoretical orientations, and helping adoptees does not necessarily require a particular theoretical approach. In fact, outcome studies show that the most effective therapy is mostly a function of whether the client and the therapist agree on the method of change, rather than the therapist's orientation. However, in working with adoptees I believe it is essential that one's theoretical framework encompass perinatal and pre-verbal loss/trauma to a sufficient extent to address the adoptee's early loss of her biological mother.

The reality of the adoptee's ongoing losses

As an adoptee grows up and develops ever-maturing emotional and cognitive capacities, she develops a deeper understanding of the meaning of being adopted. What a five-year-old understands and feels about being adopted is different than what a sixteen-year-old teenager or a thirty-six-year-old adult can understand and feel.

This awareness will include at a minimum the fact that one's biological parents did not parent them. The adoptee has probably been told different reasons for why this is so. These range from fanciful fabrications ("Your parents died in a car accident") to attempts to convey a "positive" message ("Your parents loved you very much but could not take care of you.") Be aware that many of these stories—even those told with good intentions, do not make sense when considered logically.

For example, if one's parents died in a car accident, why didn't other relatives take the adoptee in? And if the parents truly loved the adoptee, why can't they at least call on the phone or visit? Where are they now? Adoptive parents and other family members may have been ill-equipped to answer these questions and uncomfortable with them. Think about the implications for closeness in the parent/child relationship (a major template for future relationships) when your parent is either uncomfortable talking about you and/or is providing important information to you that makes no sense.

Other ongoing losses may arise in the adoptee's awareness when they realize that they have or may have other unknown biological relatives (siblings, grandparents, cousins, etc.); that their ethnic, cultural and current medical history is probably unknown; and that in all likelihood they do not have the legal right to obtain this information if it is desired. The adoptee may become gradually aware of their different, second class legal and social status.

The first biological relative an adoptee meets may be his or her own biological child. Giving birth itself may trigger an awareness of the existence of all those other biological relatives who exist, but are not known. It is often events such as birth that naturally raise awareness about one's identity, existence, and place in the "tree of humanity" that will prompt adoptees to realize their other losses. (Deaths, births, marriage, and the ubiquitous "family tree" assignment in elementary school are frequent triggers.)

Non-adoptees take for granted the existence of genetic similarities with their relatives that create closeness within families and a feeling of "home." There are characteristics which are obvious such as facial features, height and hair color, and more subtle ones like tone of voice, smell, preferences in food, literature and other interests. (When I met my birth family, I discovered one of my sisters has a laugh that sounds so much like mine that sometimes I think she is in the room when I hear myself laughing.)

These similarities anchor us to our families and in the world. Unremarkable to the non-adopted, the adoptee lacks these similarities and may feel the loss of them particularly when noticing they exist for others.

The reality of discrimination

Under the laws of many states an adoptee may be prevented from obtaining information about themselves, or face significant logistic and financial impediments to doing so. It is painful to admit, or realize, that you are treated by your government as a second class citizen. Imagine being an African American and having to tell a doctor that you don't know your medical history because the law doesn't allow black people access to their medical records. Sounds crazy, right? It's also the reality for most adoptees. It is critically important not to ignore, minimize or dismiss this reality.

Doing the work: Creating closeness to self and others in relationship

So far we've posited that an adoptee has experienced an extremely early developmental loss, as well as ongoing losses that become more conscious as the adoptee matures. Whatever feelings and thoughts the adoptee may have had about these losses have in all likelihood been denied or judged to some extent by her family, friends, and society at large. How does all of this inform us about what may come up in the adoptee's therapy about creating closeness or distance in relationship? And if you subscribe (as I do) to the belief that the therapeutic relationship is simply another relationship in which a person applies her relationships templates, what might we be looking for to happen in our relationship with the client?

My purpose here is not to describe how to work with these issues (that would take an entire book), but to suggest where to look for the work that needs to be done.

The therapist's essential hypothesis: Being adopted impacts the capacity for closeness

What hypothesis should a therapist begin with regarding the potential impact of adoption on the client's issues, particularly the issue of not being able to create the desired degree of closeness in relationships?

The therapist's hypothesis should always be that the adoption experience is relevant to the client's experience, and then only rule it out when appropriate. Assuming it is irrelevant unless explicitly brought in is unwise. This is particularly true of issues connected to closeness or distance in intimate relationships, given that rupture of close relationships essential to identity (with the birth mother, birth relatives and one's biological identity and ancestry) is the foundational experience of the adoptee.

Clients come to us with a variety of life experiences and traumas that we make note of and hold in our frame of reference. (Consider the death of a parent, a fire that burned down the family home, immigration from another country, etc.) We hold them in our awareness through the course of therapy because they are likely to be a factor in the issues the client is presenting. Being adopted is one of those particularly powerful, formative experiences.

The beginning: What is the client's level of awareness?

Adoptees, like all other clients, present on a spectrum of awareness from strong denial and unconsciousness, to highly attuned and aware.

Where is the client in her level of awareness, specifically as to the impact of being adopted on her presenting issue? How much or how little has the client considered that being adopted may have affected her psychological development? Does she believe being adopted has anything to do with her difficulty creating closeness? Why or why not?

One of our tasks as therapists is to be aware that the reasons why a client is experiencing difficulties may not be what the client identifies as the reasons. (A simple example is when a client is depressed, but does not identify the lack of close social support as a factor in her depression.) Remember that the adoptee has grown up in a culture which has denied the impact of being adopted, and she may have discounted this as well. Our job is to hold a larger awareness, not collude in denial and avoidance, and to prepare the client to explore/integrate aspects of experience that the client may not yet able to tolerate.

Allowing the politically incorrect

Saying a mother "gave away" her child is not politically correct in professional adoption circles. More correct language is that she "made a plan of adoption."

But politically correct language is rarely helpful in a therapy session. In my experience, many adoptees say that that they feel they were given away by their mothers and that they feel abandoned and rejected. This is particularly so in what we might call their younger, child mind. Here is my own description of this:

> More than twenty years ago I was chatting with one of my birth sisters about how I sometimes struggled to explain to people why my birth parents had given me away. I had searched for and found them when I was nineteen, and discovered that they had been married when I was born. My sister quipped, "Just tell them you were bad!" and howled with laughter.
>
> In that instant I felt myself split in two. One part of me howled right along with her. It was so obviously ridiculous that anyone would believe that an infant was bad. Another part contracted in pain, as if a thousand knives were stabbing my heart. That part, the younger, child mind, the vulnerable place inside of me, believed it was the truth.
>
> Children, in their natural and developmentally age-appropriate narcissism, believe what happens in the world is about them. And why would my mother give me away, unless I was bad?

You will not be able to help an adoptee if you insist on politically correct language and deny whatever language the adoptee needs to use to describe her experience, especially early on in the therapeutic relationship.

Obtaining the client's history

It is a standard part of a counseling assessment to obtain a client's family history. Be aware that simply taking a family history may be painful for an adoptee. This may be because of what the adoptee doesn't know. (e.g. "I don't know what ethnicity I am.") It may be painful because of information they do know. (e.g. "My mother was date raped and couldn't bear to parent me." Or, "My mother's parents, my grandparents, forced her to give me away.") Or it may touch upon what an adoptee consciously or unconsciously fears or believes. (e.g. "My mother gave me away because she didn't love me.") Later on, knowing these facts may help you and the client discover patterns in creating closeness and distance in relationships.

It is entirely possible that you will be the first person the adoptee talks to about her experience of being adopted. Frequently adoptees have suffered significant isolation around the experience of being adopted due to denial, avoidance, judgment, or other negative and silencing reactions from family, friends, society, or the mental health system. It is very common for the adoptee to have lived her entire life in at least some degree of silence regarding being adopted. They may discuss being adopted in a "reporting" fashion, without emotion.

What the non-adopted consider basic, normal questioning about oneself may have been taboo or difficult topics in the adoptee's childhood home. (e.g. "Which relatives do I look like?" "What was it like for you the night I was born?" "Where do our people come from?") Adoptive parents' verbal and non-verbal reactions to these kinds of questions may have conveyed fear or shame. For example, an adoptee's questions about the circumstances of her birth may touch an adoptive parent's pain around infertility, or fear that the child might want to look for or would prefer the birth parent. A child could interpret these reactions as her questions

(or herself) are wrong, rather than having something to
do with the parent.

Try to get a sense of how the adoptee's family
(including not only parents but grandparents and other
extended family members) did, and did not, discuss
adoption. What wasn't talked about is usually more
important than what was. Notice whether the
information may be available and the adoptee has not
asked for it (e.g. information which may be in the
adoptive parent's possession), or whether access to it may
have been denied (e.g. the adoptive parent refused to
provide it).

Has the adoptee searched for her biological
family? Why or why not? Where are they in the process
of searching? If she has searched, what was the result?
Search itself is an extensive subject, however one of the
most important psychological issues for search is the
specter of a "second rejection" by the birth
mother/family should they be found and refuse contact.
Most adoptees have considerable fear about this
possibility. Tremendous pain is experienced by the tiny
minority of adoptees for whom this actually happens.

Relationship history

Get as much information as possible about how
the client begins, or avoids getting into, relationships.
Also get as much information as possible about how the
client ends, or does not end, relationships. (The kinds of
things to notice are rushing into relationships; an inability
to end inappropriate relationships; abrupt endings;
walking away or pre-emptive rejection.) Does any of this
track, re-enact, or mirror the adoptee's adoption loss or
experience?

Look for the adoptee's conscious or unconscious
expectation that relationships cannot tolerate certain
things to be spoken. (e.g. "My mom gets so
uncomfortable when I ask about my adoption: I better

not ask any more questions.") A child's take-away from
this experience may be that relationships can't tolerate
certain pieces of "me," or that it's dangerous or
unacceptable to express my needs. Beliefs like these, of
course, create distance instead of closeness in
relationships.

Belonging and not belonging

As Robert Frost says, home is "When you have to
go there, they have to take you in." Yet the adoptee's
experience is that the home (viz.—with her biological
mother/family) is where she was not taken in.
Alternatively, the adoptive home is where someone
"chose" to take you in. This is not the same as having a
place where you have the right to belong. Conscious or
unconsciously, being chosen creates the possibility that
you can be "unchosen."

Can the adoptee feel like she "belongs" in a group
or in a relationship (including her relationship with you,
the therapist)? Look for her to have difficulty processing
feelings related to (real or perceived) rejection and
abandonment. Is she so guarded against the possibility of
a relationship creating a future rejection or abandonment,
that she avoids letting herself get close to people?
Avoidance of connection tends to recreate the very
experience she is afraid of: feeling like she doesn't belong
with and is not connected to others.

Having an external home (physically and in secure
relationships with family members) creates a feeling of
"home" inside us. When we feel we belong, like we are at
"home" with another or with ourselves, we feel
physiologically and emotionally regulated. Does she feel
regulated or dysregulated most of the time? Are there any
relationships in her life that feel like "home"?

What experiences (sensory, physical, emotional,
and cognitive) can't she tolerate? How about emotions
like grief, anger, fear? Look for patterns that suggest what

she finds unbearable is related to the reality of loss and relinquishment, or fear of rejection or abandonment. Creating distance in relationship often is a reflection of the distance we maintain from our internal pain. I can't get close to **you** if I can't get close to **me**.

Pay attention to how the client feels about you. Does she expect to be turned away from you, either consciously or unconsciously? Is she waiting for you to kick her out of therapy if she does something wrong?

Expect her to be looking for you to mother her, and perhaps afraid of your rejection at the same time. Does she attach too quickly and too easily? Or not attach at all? Expect the client to push you away, perhaps while also clinging to you (indicating her confusion about boundaries.) Where do I end, and where do you begin?

As always we have to watch our own countertransference to clients about intimacy, closeness and distance. How do you react to clients who expect you to reject or abandon them? This dynamic is likely to be particularly active with adoptees.

What doesn't the adoptee talk about, particularly around the reality of her adoption? Are there aspects of her adoption experience that she can't or won't talk about, or perhaps even think about? Can the therapeutic relationship tolerate her bringing her full self, feelings and thoughts about being adopted into it? Or does she believe this will threaten her right to belong in therapy? Is it dangerous for her to express her needs about being adopted?

Loyalty binds: Being forced to choose

Look for loyalty binds that might recapitulate the implied conflict between having both an adoptive mother and a birth mother. Can she have more than one mother, or more than one family? Does she feels like she is betraying her adoptive mother/family if she needs to know about or have a connection with her biological family?

This either/or loyalty bind tends to be very strong in adoptees and manifests in other relationships, including but not limited to the therapeutic relationship. Can I have a relationship with you and be myself at the same time? It may be useful to draw an analogy in your own mind to children of divorce being torn between loyalty to their mother and their father. Must I choose between my parents (viz.—between my adoptive and birth families) and deny part of myself, or can I have both of them (and all of me)?

Healing loyalty binds results in a both/and rather than an either/or mentality. I have both an adoptive family and a birth family. I have my own needs and can acknowledge your needs. I can love myself and love you.

Grief, grief, and more grief

When everything else is cleared out of the way, what is left over is simply grief. Grief over the myriad of past losses, and those that may be ongoing. Grief doesn't need "therapy." It needs support, love, compassion, space, and time.

Finally: Transcending and healing

What will closeness in relationship look like for an adoptee? Well, pretty much like it looks for everyone else! But specifically, an adoptee will feel like she belongs to herself and that all parts of her are conscious and accepted. She will have, and continue to cultivate, a deep love for herself. It involves transcending the "child mind" that may believe she is unworthy or bad because she was "given away." She will not feel caught in loyalty binds, where she must sacrifice or deny parts of herself or her feelings in order to be in close relationships with others.

These kinds of statements reflect healing and an increased capacity for closeness:

"I belong."

"I am not bad."

"I am worthwhile."

"I matter."

"My needs and feelings matter."

"I can bring all of who I am to this relationship."

"I can be close to you without betraying or sacrificing myself."

"I don't need to pretend I am someone I am not."

"I have the right to know the truth about myself."

Don't forget it's not ALL about being adopted

Don't forget that every adoptee has **had a childhood** and an adulthood.

The biological child of a narcissistic mother will be affected in certain anticipated ways. An adopted child of the same mother will be also wounded in those ways, but the effects will take place layered on top of the reality of being adopted. Every adoptee, and every adoptee's therapist, needs to keep the question in mind, "Is this about being adopted, or is it simply my life?"

Homeward Bound

When I was in my forties my adoptive mother and I were having lunch and the discussion turned to adoption. She confided in me that she was always aware that I had suffered a great loss before I came into her life. With a touch of determination in her voice she shared that knowing that, she had tried as hard as she could to keep anything bad from happening to me ever again. Of course that wasn't, and never could be, the case. But I was stunned and deeply moved that she had known, that she had understood. That she had some glimmer of an idea of what I had gone through as a tiny infant.

As therapists we are in a position to know, even if our adoptee clients don't, that they have suffered great loss. The loss of a fundamental, foundational place of home. That both their willingness and capacity to create closeness in their relationships with others has in all likelihood been impacted by this loss. Our work is to help each adoptee we work with to become more aware of her defenses, belief systems, or other limitations that arose as a result, and to take the necessary healing steps to fully restore the capacity for intimacy. We must help them navigate their unreality, pain, loyalty binds, identity issues, and feelings such as grief and anger that will restore the full capacity of their hearts. Home, after all, is where the heart is.

Author's Note: The use of the feminine pronoun throughout is for ease of reading. It is worth noting that the vast majority of my adoptee clients have been women, however, a discussion of the probable reasons for this would require its own chapter.

Reference

Fessler, Ann. *The Girls Who Went Away: The Hidden History of Women Who Surrendered Children for Adoption in the Decades Before Rose v. Wade*. New York: Penguin Books, 2006.

* * *

Karen Caffrey, LPC, JD is a Licensed Professional Counselor, a certified Somatic Experiencing Practitioner, a writer, a reunited adoptee, and an attorney. She has a private psychotherapy practice in West Hartford, Connecticut, and invites you to visit her at *www.karencaffrey.com* and on Facebook, "Karen Caffrey Counseling." One of her specialties is counseling adult adoptees. Karen is also President of Access Connecticut Now, Inc., a grassroots organization that successfully lobbied for a 2014 law that has restored the right of post-1983 adoptees to access their original birth certificates. Karen and Access Connecticut remain committed to restoring the right of all Connecticut adoptees to know the truth about their origins.

Chapter 7—Perspective of an Adoptee Conceived by Rape

By Kristi Lado

If you open any adoptee self-help book you're likely to see a section addressing self-worth and "lovability." Most will pose a question along the lines of, "What could a tiny baby have done that would cause a mother to reject her?" The answer the author is looking for is "nothing," and this is supposed to help us "reframe" our childhood notion that we were given up because of some horrible flaw.

My answer to the question is different than most adoptees. It isn't so much what I *did* but what I *am*. I share DNA with the man who raped my natural mother. The flaw, at times, seems very real. It has undoubtedly played a role in every major interaction involving my adoption.

The family secret

I was not informed of my conception circumstances until I announced that I was searching in my twenties. My adoptive mother conveyed this information via email ... a message that I unfortunately read at work.

Naturally, I was hurt and angry. When I asked my mother why she didn't tell me sooner, I didn't receive an apology, but a flippant dismissal, "You couldn't have handled it as a teenager! We were just trying to protect you! Besides, the adoption lawyer didn't believe her [my birth mother] anyway." I knew darned well it wasn't about my feelings at all.

My parents hadn't told the extended family either. I don't believe this was so much out of respect for me, but out of shame and denial. My adoptive mother was happy living in her fantasy bubble. She didn't want to acknowledge I came from someone else, let alone existed because of a very horrible act.

A reluctant reunion

I barely had time to process my conception story before finding my birth mother. When I explained how much meeting her would mean to me she wrote, "I feel like a person who's been told that their kidney is the only match for a dying person. Do I want to give up a kidney and live with what that entails? No. Do I want to be the kind of person who would refuse? No." There was zero empathy. Only cold truths: "I never for one second allowed myself to love you except in a universal way. I didn't touch, or even look at you when you were born." She explained that only her mother knew I existed, and that I was not to contact anyone in her (my) family.

She agreed to meet, but my impression was that she did so out of a sense of duty. Her visible flinch when we first laid eyes on each other signaled what we both knew: it was obvious that I inherited most of my features from my genetic father. I felt … *responsible*. I wanted to make it better. I wanted to hug her, but I knew she didn't want to be touched.

My natural mom never wanted children. She explained that her decision to carry her pregnancy to term was a question of, "How would I feel if I allowed you to live, versus how would I feel if I had an abortion?" She said that my genetic father was "an acquaintance, but not a romantic interest." She had reported the rape, but did not take it any further when she found out she was pregnant.

As a child I was told she gave me up because I would remind her of *him*, and she didn't want to take that out on me. My natural mom knew herself well. There were many mixed signals throughout my visit with her. Sometimes she'd ask questions as if she really wanted to get to know me, and other times she took passive-aggressive shots at my expense. She hated that I cared about my beginnings and attempted to convince me that they "weren't important."

There was one brief instant that the walls came down and we had a very sacred, tearful exchange where she expressed no regrets. We discovered striking similarities and finished each other's sentences. I felt the bond I knew I was missing my entire life, but it was all too brief. As the visit ended, she informed me that she didn't want a relationship.

She agreed to scant communication after meeting, and I forced the other shoe to drop after working up the nerve to ask the name of my genetic father. She said that she had "blotted it from her memory" and that I needed "help for my obsession." She told me I was hurting because I was beginning to realize what I'd "done to myself." I was commanded to leave her alone. Forever. She stated emphatically that she had "moved on." But moving on is much different from healing.

"Therapy"

I spent many days after my reunion collapsed in a heap on the floor. At that time I was very involved in adoptee rights and support organizations, but no longer had the energy. Therapists trained in adoptee issues almost didn't exist back then. I sought out a therapist that took my insurance ... she was the first of three. One blank stare after another made me feel crazier for grieving the loss of a human being that I "didn't know." I gave up, shut down, and got on with life. I asked my doctor for an antidepressant because I just needed to *function*.

For the next ten years, I numbed myself to all-things-adoption. My husband's job took us to a far-away town. Having my children was a happy distraction. It seemed I had mostly "gotten over" the bad feelings in the sense that they didn't hinder my everyday functioning. I coped the way I was expected to cope: the way my birth mother did.

Every-so-often, in crept the questions. What could I have said, done, or been for her to have wanted me in her life? Deep down I knew I could have won the Nobel Prize and it wouldn't have made a difference. The "flaw" as she saw it, the one awful fact I couldn't change, was what mattered most to her.

"Therapy," part two

Our move back to Eastern Pennsylvania renewed my interest in my biological family, a "coming home" of sorts. It was eleven years post-reunion, and I began to research my mother's family tree with earnest.

My husband and I travelled to the family's home town in West Virginia and visited a number of grave sites, including those of my biological grandparents. It hit home how much I was missing. My grandmother, the only one that knew I existed, died before I could meet her. It was not lost on me that I was learning more about the dead relatives than the living ones. How many family stories did I not know, which would die with my mother, aunt, uncles, and cousins? I finally worked up the nerve to look up my extended family members, including two uncles and an aunt. The uncles both lived in my home state of Pennsylvania, one about forty minutes from my home.

It triggered the next avalanche. I took a massive step forward. I called my biological mother and expressed interest in meeting the rest of my biological family. This went about as well as I expected. Her words, "YOU ARE VIOLATING ME!" will ring in my ears for the rest of my life. I managed to squeak out, "That's not my intention," and the conversation ended.

All of the pent-up grief I was carrying around erupted. I sought out the help of someone who specialized in adoptee therapy and Post-Traumatic Stress Disorder (PTSD). It was so difficult to describe how I felt, she handed me a list of feelings so I could point to and articulate them: Guilt-ridden, powerless, despicable, unimportant, despairing, helpless, inferior, panicked, tormented, heartbroken, anguished ... *a disappointment.*

I realized I'd been holding back my pain because I didn't believe it was as important or legitimate as my mother's, *and I'd allowed her to convince me of that.* I was angry that she felt entitled to withhold my genetic father's name and dictate that I could not contact my own biological family. I was hurt that I was expected to go away and pretend I didn't exist.

One-by-one, I took every negative feeling on the list and "replaced" it with something positive. A reoccurring theme was, "I am strong." I was brave enough to face my fears and to be honest. This is the type of person I wanted to be. I refused to cower in an invisible place because someone thought I belonged there.

The most pressing matter I wanted to work out with the therapist was, ethically, how would I feel going against my birth mother's wishes? I said I felt like I'd backed a raped woman into a corner, to which she replied, "It's a self-made corner, Kristi. She chose to keep you a secret. The question is, What is your ultimate goal in contacting them?" Ultimate goal? I would have been happy to have contact with one biological relative, even if we only spoke once a year.

I find, "Why do you want to know your biological family?" to be such an inane question, I have yet to find a satisfactory canned answer for someone who would ask it. In knowing them and learning more about my roots, I would hope to know myself better. I received some missing pieces from my birth mother, and they were so validating. I couldn't stand the thought of allowing my relatives to die off without ever making an attempt to reach out.

In our last conversation my birth mother asked, "Don't you have a family who loves you? Isn't that enough?" If I'd had my wits about me at the time I would have answered that my yearnings aren't for a lack of love. I value my biological family because I can't help but seeing them as having the potential to be as good as my relationships with my adoptive aunts, uncles and cousins. I refuse to choose hierarchy of who's more important, nor will I discount one because the other exists.

When someone's biological connections are severed, it is a serious loss that needs to be recognized and respected. I felt terrible for my birth mother, but I felt like I was living under the terms and conditions of a contract I never signed.

The family pariah

I drafted letters to some of my relatives, hands and knees shaking as I sent them. Weeks passed. The slip with my aunt's signature arrived. Her writing was similar to my natural mother's. I heard nothing. It's been about a year as of this writing.

I understand that they're only trying to protect someone they love. Part of me feels angry that my birth mother obviously influenced them. How dare she be ashamed of me, and by extension my children? Another part feels sorry for her. Her attempt to control the situation is indicative of the last thing she deserves to feel: shame.

I read somewhere that most decisions in life boil down to a choice between love and fear. My natural mother and I remind each other of what we most fear. In standing up for myself, my biggest fear (familial rejection) has happened, but it has also been conquered. She/they chose fear over love. I'm proud that I did the opposite. I mustered the strength to risk reliving such devastating loss, and in doing so I've stood up for my self-worth.

What I mourn most is, had she chosen love, it could have been very healing for both of us.

The peanut gallery

When Laura sent her request for submissions, this book was humorously titled, "Does Adoption Make us Crazy?" Most adoptees who have been through the emotional wringer of search and reunion would give that an emphatic, "YES!" I believe what is truly crazy-making about being adopted and/or rape-conceived is the severe lack of understanding of either scenario.

I'm very open with people about my story, but this comes at the price of fielding wildly ignorant commentary. To an extent, people are only regurgitating the ideas that are so prevalent in our culture. The language used to describe people in my situation is very dehumanizing: "rape baby," "product," "demon spawn," and worse.

Some try to dictate how I should interpret my experience. "Just be grateful for your life!" "At least you had a good home." These statements are indicative of how people, almost on a subconscious level, see adoptees (especially those in my situation) as being a charity case and somehow beneath them. They are not speaking of normal healthy gratitude a person feels for life in general. This type of gratitude-speak implies that we should *know our place* and be subservient because we were "spared." They could just as easily have been talking about a dog someone rescued from the pound.

Others see us as political pawns. "Thank God she didn't abort you!" "You are why these babies need to be born! It's a child, not a choice!" (Actual things that have been said to me.) The tone is often self-congratulatory, as if the pro-life movement single-handedly saved my life. To these people, my only value is to be the poster child for a political cause. I answer to this nonsense the same way every time: *I don't believe in forcing a woman by law to carry any pregnancy to term. If I was able to be with my mother in spirit at the time she had to make that decision, I would have supported her either way.* In reality the pro-life movement, a major proponent of sealed records, has done more to hurt adoptees' well-being than it has helped.

All of it takes a form of cultural gas-lighting that undermines and devalues the realities of the people living the experience. Every time I hear a dismissive platitude or disempowering statement, I can't help but ask myself: Would anyone in their right mind dare try to tell a raped woman how to feel about being raped? Why is it acceptable to tell the resulting child how to feel about how they came into the world?

You may be thinking, "Sticks and stones. Ignore 'em and forget it." Unfortunately, it's not that simple. These pervasive attitudes not only affect the way we are treated personally, but they also (unfortunately) translate into public policy.

Human rights

As of this writing, HB 162, a bill that would allow adoptees access to their original birth certificates is under review by the Senate Committee of Aging and Youth in Pennsylvania. The rape scenario has been used as a major excuse to kill the bill, or add a stipulation that birth parents could choose to have their names withheld from their children.

The Pennsylvania Coalition Against Rape, PA NOW, and even the PA ACLU (an organization supposedly dedicated to equal treatment under the law) oppose equal access to original birth certificates. In the ACLU's testimony letter regarding HB 162, they state,

"In many cases, the need for privacy protects both the adoptee and the biological parent, especially in cases where a biological parent was involved in an act of violence and/or rape." In other words, they see it as perfectly acceptable to treat a rape-conceived child as if they are the perpetrator. I found it especially insulting that they purport to be "protecting" people like me by arguing that we should be kept from the truth of our existence.

For supposedly being so progressive, all of these groups harbor very shame-based attitudes against the rape-conceived. Our rights are seen as a game of *Let's Make a Deal.* They want you to live ... but only in accordance with someone else's emotional comfort level.

They are essentially arguing for a woman's right to live in denial of her trauma at her child's expense. Is this society's idea of emotional health? I don't believe this policy respects the woman or the child. Sealing the records of an innocent human being to "protect" a raped woman treats her as if she is a perpetual victim. Don't get me wrong. I don't believe anyone should be forced to have a relationship that makes them uncomfortable, but certainly this can be handled by simply saying "no," adult to adult, rather than expecting the government to micromanage the relationship.

Natural mothers in an unnatural situation

At the start of this writing, I asked myself what (if any) difference is there in the mother/child dynamics between a conceived-under-normal-circumstances adoption and one where the child was conceived by rape?

I'm not a therapist, so I can only answer with personal observations. In some ways, they are almost identical, but with (I believe) an added layer of trauma and stress for the natural mother and baby. The trauma of rape and carrying an unwanted pregnancy adds to the ambivalence some mothers feel and the tendency to project unresolved negative feelings on the child. On the other hand, I have seen rape-conceived adoptees reunite with their natural mothers and have very fulfilling relationships.

So why such differences in how the child is received in reunion? In my experience, the biggest factor is the degree to which the mother has worked through her trauma. Denial is often the brain's default when faced with a life-threatening situation. It can save our lives by allowing us to function in the moment of a threat. Immediately afterwards, its numbing properties might be the only thing keeping us from jumping off a bridge. However, when a mother uses denial as the long term coping mechanism, contact from a relinquished child often brings about a flood of unresolved emotion. A mother in denial will often treat her child as the cause of her upset. She will reject the child because she is rejecting the feelings. It is often the only way she knows how to cope.

Values and family culture definitely play a role. (I'm going to go out on a limb and guess that my mother was raised with the good ol' fashioned Catholic "pretend it never happened" technique for handling unpleasant events in life.)

Much of it is also the X-factor which is individual's personality and psychological makeup. Some women seem to be able to completely separate the event from the child almost instantly. Others can't seem to help seeing them as one and the same.

The trauma is real for all mothers of loss, but certainly increases exponentially for those who conceived from rape. Even today, finding a therapist who is truly competent to handle this situation can be daunting.

To believe or not to believe?

This question is posed pretty often to people in my situation, so it must be addressed. Do I believe my birth mother was raped? My honest answer to that question is: mostly, yes.

Based on the look in my mother's eyes and her reactions to meeting me, I believe what I saw. The tiny shadow of doubt comes from life experience. Since lies are almost always an inherent part of a closed adoption, part of me will never believe what I'm told by *anyone* with absolute certainty. When someone attempts to exert a hyper level of control over the situation like my birth mother did, it gives me a nagging feeling of suspicion. I don't think she lied about the rape, but I wouldn't be surprised if there's something more to the story.

Bottom line is I have to believe it for my sanity. If I go too far down the road of, "Maybe she lied and there's a perfectly nice bio father and family out there that don't know I exist," it becomes an unproductive psychological rabbit hole.

Thoughts on my genetic father

How do I feel about sharing half my genetic makeup with a rapist? The "ick" factor is hard to deny. What personality traits do we share? Am I "part evil" like in some horror movie? Is it my destiny to be burdened with the "sins of my father" in some twisted biblical sense?

In being rejected by my biological family, I will always live out the legacy of what this man did. I regret being too afraid to upset my birth mother to ask more about him. Was he was mentally ill or just an entitled jerk? Surely I've inherited more than physical traits from him. I will always wonder what genetics I'm carrying around and potentially passing on to my children.

These thoughts will always operate in the background, but I keep them in check because ultimately the actions of this man do not dictate who I am and the kind of person I choose to be.

How and when to tell

Adoptive parents may think that excluding rape from their child's story will save her from feeling pain. I can tell you from experience, lying-by-omission will only compound this pain when she does find out. Notice I said "when" not "if." The truth will always come out, whether the child finds out from researching her adoption or from her original mother.

I would advise adoptive parents to start with a "soft truth." Perhaps something like, "Your natural mother did not want a relationship with your father." As your child gets older and asks more questions, you may expand on that truth, maybe adding that he did not treat her very well. In my opinion, kids should hear the full truth by adolescence… perhaps twelve or thirteen, depending on maturity level.

Everybody deserves full knowledge of their origins. Trusting that the child can handle the truth of her conception sends a clear message that parents respect her and her ability to process this reality.

What worked for me

As you may have guessed from my opening paragraph, I've found adoptee self-help books mostly useless. Most of them are very good at pointing out the problems, but fail miserably at offering any viable solution. I don't necessarily blame the authors. This is such an under-researched subject that all of us are feeling around in the dark.

What worked for me is not necessarily going to work for everyone, but I'll list what I found useful:

Seek out a therapist that specializes in adoptee issues. I cannot stress enough how important it is to find a therapist that "gets it." Do yourself a favor and pre-interview potential therapists before you spend a red cent on someone that only makes you feel worse.

Get help for Post-Traumatic Stress. Most of my PTSD work involved identifying my feelings. As simple as it sounds, actually looking at that list of feelings and pointing out specifics helped untangle a massive ball of negative feelings I was carrying around. Free-floating emotion turned concrete and somehow more manageable. I was able to look at each feeling and think, "Is this rational? What is the reality?" When done in combination with EMDR (Eye Movement Desensitization and Reprocessing) therapy, this can work wonders.

Seek out a support group. Communicating with others who have had similar experiences does well to eliminate feeling isolated and misunderstood.

As for the specific situation of being rape-conceived, much of what exists focuses on using our stories for a political agenda rather than actual emotional support. I'm happy to say I was able to team up with those of similar mindset to create an online support group called C.A.R.E.S. (Conceived After Rape Empowerment and Support).

Continued healing

Healing from adoption issues is a lifelong process. I will always be devastated that I'll probably never have a connection with my family of origin. But I've learned that it is possible to have the emotions without allowing them to control me.

I read somewhere that the best form of therapy is giving others what you always needed and never received.

In sharing my experience, I hope I'm able to give others the empathy and understanding that I'd never gotten.

As of this writing, I've regained my momentum and rejoined the adoptee community with renewed passion. I've become politically active again, speaking out for adoptees' rights to identity, specifically original birth certificates and adoption records.

I write not to define myself as a "child of rape" but to affirm my humanity. I'm not wallowing or ignoring. I'm taking action. I've been able to crawl out from under the emotional rubble, stand on top with my head held high, and see it clearly for what it is. This is true strength.

* * *

Kristi Lado was adopted through the closed domestic system in Pennsylvania. Formerly an associate producer for cable TV's *Forensic Files*, she has since become an independent writer and advocate for open records. Kristi has served as a board member for Adoption Forum of Philadelphia and volunteers for Pennsylvania Adoptee Rights (PAR). She recently co-founded C.A.R.E.S., an online support forum for those conceived by rape, and blogs about adoption issues at www.Aquarian Adoptee.com.

Chapter 8—The Transracial Adoptee and Body Dysmorphia

By Lucy Chau Lai-Tuen

The true legacy of being a transracial adoptee didn't really hit me until I was approaching fifty. Thinking about it, that's a hell of a long time to spend not knowing, deep down, who or what you are. Mis-quoting a very famous United Kingdom advertisement, designed to discourage people from buying puppies as Christmas presents:

A transracial adoptee is for life.

Being a transracial adoptee is a lifelong condition. Once you have been transracially adopted there is no going back. This action cannot be reversed. Neither is it something that can be discarded. It will remain an essential part of me until the day I die. For that reason I often refer to myself as, 'a recovering transracial adoptee.' It interlocks and interfaces with me, my identity, self-perception and the assumptions that many in the wider society still have of me as an East Asian. To me that meant dealing with loss. After having first accepted that I had suffered a loss. Dealing with the trauma. The baggage, the racial discrimination, the cultural dislocation, and the linguistic disenfranchisement. Along with the usual challenges that a person of color, growing up in a Western, Caucasian society is faced with on a daily basis.

Each of those aspects has become an integral, subconscious part of my being. I now embrace the loss, the challenges, the anger, the raw, sometimes bitter emotions, that occasionally surface out of the blue, but that's all part and parcel of being a transracial adoptee. I now appreciate all aspects of being a transracial adoptee. The Yin and Yang, by having accepted the things that I cannot change. Having the courage to change the things that I can and the wisdom to know the difference.

My life and what it is has become is a direct result of having been transracially adopted. Having been culturally displaced. I was linguistically and racially disenfranchised. For a long time "identity intolerant," though the intolerance was not on my part. But typically came, *comes* from those within the wider society. Even, sad to say, a small minority from my own ethnic and racial background. Each adoptee's story is different and unique. Some experience transracial adoption as a life-affirming positive. Others, as a negative and profoundly damaging intervention, some, experience both negative and positive. Whatever our individual experiences are, they are no less valid or true than the next person's. An adoptee's life experiences cover the full range just as any other person's life does.

We must all respect the adoptee's experience. We do what is best for us at the time we are in and at the stage we have reached. Adoption is a lifelong condition.

For me, finding out, understanding, who and what I was, what I am, has always been a driving force. From a very early age I knew that there was something, "not quite right" about me and the people that surrounded me whom I referred to as family.

> *So much of what is best in us is bound up in our love of family, that it remains the measure of our stability because it measures our sense of loyalty.*
> —Haniel Long

If Haniel Long is right, where does this leave me? My cultural DNA is missing some essential strands. Transracial adoption tried to graft me onto another existence. For me the transplant wasn't successful. Like a human rejecting a donor organ, I found myself rejected by the very culture and society that had adopted me.

I was brought up by a white, middle class family, with all privileges. But with no realistic expectations of ever being able to take advantage of such privileges. Why? Color, ethnicity, and race. No matter what I did, who I became, I would never ever be able to change the color of my skin or my ethnicity. I would always be an East Asian.

Looking back on my early life, I was growing up in physical, cultural, and racial isolation. Is it any wonder that for the first six years of my life I thought that I was white? One of the greatest challenges that face any transracially adopted child is the possible lack of visible social and cultural mirrors both at home and in the wider society. Family-wise, I had no such mirrors. I grew up unable to see my own reflection in those who lived around or in the community. I had no idea how I might physically develop. If you isolate a person from their culture, their racial and ethnic roots, what is that saying to the child? My adoptive parents took the accepted Sixties view. A clean break from the child's past, sever any connection or reference to the child's country of birth. They did exactly so, because that's what they were told to do. But by doing so they were undervaluing, saying to that child that a part who and what you are is of no importance. My race and ethnicity were reduced to nothing more than a set of stereotypes, grotesque and racially inaccurate tropes, that were common place and popular during the early Sixties in Britain. By refusing to acknowledge the existence of people like me. By writing people like me out of British culture and only allowing reference to East Asians in factually incorrect parameters, I continued to be perceived as a minority. I was never accepted, never understood because there was no interest

in trying to understand how I felt or why I felt the way
that I did. I was doomed to an existence which offered
no hope of emancipation and was therefore enslaved
politically, socially, and culturally. Keeping me as the
"other," the outsider, the foreigner.

I'm still trying to untangle what the cultural and
linguistic displacement actually did to me as a child and
how it has affected me now as a mature adult. Each year
goes by and I uncover another impacted and distorted
strata that transracial adoption has bequeathed me.

To think for the first few years of my life, until I
was six, I thought that I was white. I was culturally,
racially, ethnically, and linguistically confused. A cultural
anorexic. Looking into a mirror and seeing a face that
wasn't mine. Seeing a blond-haired and blue-eyed kid
gazing back.

I've written and spoken about this in public on
numerous occasions and will continue to do so, as this
encapsulates my experience. Highlighting the danger and
harm that can result from disembodied transracial
adoption, and all that is negative and unacceptable about
viewing transracial adoption as some form of evangelical
act of salvation and rescue. How many times and oft
must adoptees hear the remnants of Eurocentric and
Western colonialism as it filters through and trickles
down into the act of adoption? It would appear that
Colonial expansionist superiority is hard-wired into the
unconscious thinking of many Caucasians and Western
societies. When I was adopted, "Empire," though
physically diminished, was mentally still in the forebrain
of many a British citizen.

I was three when I was taken by my adoptive
mother, who was a primary school teacher, and put on
display, as the object of a "bring and tell" session, a
popular educational activity in schools during the Sixties.
Children would bring in an object, stand in front of their
class and tell them all about it. I was the first and I hope
the last child that was ever brought in and put on show as
an object for "bring and tell." I was dressed in the clothes

that I had worn on the journey from the orphanage in Hong Kong to the United Kingdom. At the age of three, the clothes finally fit me properly. I was plonked on a desk for all to see. I was poked, prodded, and giggled at. Surrounded by kids pulling their eyelids back and talking at me in a fake and exaggerated accent. Some kids even licking their fingers and wiping my face, to see if the "yellowness" would rub off. I have never forgotten the details of that incident. In fact I think I would be hard pressed to forget that day. It was the beginning of the end in terms of the relationship with my adoptive mother and family.

At the tender age of three I learnt in a brutal, embarrassing, and derogatory fashion that I was different. That my "difference" was more than just skin deep. My adoptive parents refused to talk about such subjects. In true British post-war tradition, they remained resolutely silent with a stiff upper lip. Children were seen and but not heard. When an elder and better told you off or instructed you to do something, there was no room for questions or cavaliers. The age of corporal punishment domestically and in the education system was still an accepted and universally applied form of discipline.

So at three I experienced a major revelation and it would be the first of many major and minor unpleasant realizations that occurred in the school playground. As parents held on, that bit firmer, to their child as I walked past. Or being subject to a complete stranger yelling things at me on the street in a fake Chinese accent. All of this was kept well under control whilst I was a child. As is the case with children in their formative years, they are controlled and heavily influenced by their family. Being able to find and understand who they are, by seeing themselves as individuals, but also finding themselves in the eyes, the features, and the faces of everyone that surrounded them. I did not have that luxury either in the home or out in the wider world of the local community. As a baby all was well. I was small, "cute," and a novelty. As a toddler I was a "China doll." The older I got, the

more I tried to fit into the family and society. The more
of an outsider I became. But as soon as I started school
the real journey began. It's a journey that every child
embarks upon, that of self-discovery, the emergence of
one's own identity. The commencement of placing your
feet firmly into the ancestral mix as you combine and
become yet another branch of your family, your culture,
your heritage, and your race. But I had nothing in which
to embed myself.

It's only now with the luxury of hindsight and
age, that I can look back on my childhood, teenage years,
and early adulthood without recoiling.

I think that I was ill for the majority of my
formative, teenage, and young adult years. My
"illness" was only picked up towards the end, when it
significantly manifested and could be labelled as "a
nervous breakdown" when I was in my late teens.

I had "left" home; I was at college and working
three jobs: early morning cleaner, occasional lunch time
and weekend bar staff, and evening noodle cook in a busy
central London restaurant. Somehow I managed to find
the time to study, attend college and work, without for
the most part being late or falling asleep during the day.
But what I did do was cry a lot, for no apparent reason.
Not just the odd sob here and there. I'd cry for minutes
inconsolably, tears and emotions so deep, so dark, there
were times that I thought it would never stop. I would
literally cry myself to sleep. For the entire three years that
I was at drama school, I was an insomniac. I'd get at best
four to maybe six hours of sleep per week. When I wasn't
sleeping, I was crying. But when I did stop there was no
release. I just felt bereft, empty, and at a loss. Things got
really bad when I was in my second year; during one
recess I seriously contemplated suicide. I sat for hours
perched on a window sill of the room that I was renting.
Three floors up, an old Victorian house divided up into
bedsits for rent. I honestly cannot remember now what
stopped me from just letting go. Perhaps it was the sunny
day, maybe it was the fact that I'd been sitting there for

hours and if I'd really, really meant to let go, I'd have done it the moment that I'd swung my legs out over the window sill. I remember feeling the sun on my skin, the birds singing, me just being empty and drained, inside sucked dry of anything. Whatever it was, whatever the internal motivation, the internal conversation in the back of my head, the will to carry on won out that day. Not long after that I started seeing a therapist, and my long road to recovery began. My road to understanding the ghosts and the blackness began.

Winding the clock back, I returned to the moment that I was separated from all that should have grounded and influenced me. That is the moment that I believe I became susceptible to internal illness and identity dysmorphia. I think that it's only natural as a child to want to fit in, to "fix" how you appear to the world outside so that you can get along and be happy. But when that natural desire becomes a preoccupation, when it begins to unconsciously take over your life, it becomes problematic if not addressed. It's probably indicative of a more deeply rooted problem. The desire that I had to physically fit in and to actually try and do things to myself to make that physical fit more appropriate to the society and community that I was growing up in became an unconscious "habit." I lost for a considerable period of time the ability to see myself in the mirror as I actually was. I was the equivalent of an identity anorexic. But instead of food, identity and appearance were my trigger—*Angennisi Nervosa*. I was suffering from what I have coined, "Identity Dysmorphia." I find the following phrase intriguing, 'you are what you eat,' which will resonate with the anorexic in a way that those of us who do not suffer from this condition can never quite begin to understand, even though we may sympathize. For the *Angennisi Nervosa*, the suffering it is exactly the same. It's not food, but racial—self, image, and identity. It's a dislocation from the physical and the physiognomic representation of one's race, ethnicity, and cultural identity. Only there is no sympathy from the wider society. There is no real recognition, even within the health community of what this condition can do to the individual. I also believe it is a condition that would more commonly, if not "exclusively" be found amongst transracial adoptees, and those who have grown up as multiple and habitually transracially fostered children.

It is very difficult, maybe nigh on impossible, for a Caucasian person in the West to understand and appreciate what it is to be without a grounded identity. Many of those who criticize the logistics and politics of identity and belonging come from a place in society where they have never had to question their position in life. They know exactly who they are and where they come from. Their place in the world is reinforced by their genes, their familial ties, and the culture and its reflections via art and literature. These facets and depictions all bolster and confirm their place and belonging. So it's easy from a position of security to poo-poo the idea that identity is a human construct that has little or no value. They have never had to question—and in turn are never questioned about, their provenance or their identity and roots.

The dysmorphia element for me took the form of physically trying to "fix" my appearance. It meant that if I was ever going to stand any chance of physically fitting in, I would have to change the shape of my eyes and nose. To this end I religiously went to bed with an old-fashioned wooden clothes peg wedged onto my nose. Quite how I thought this was going to produce bone growth, I'm not sure. But in my defense I was all of four-years-old. I also persevered for an equally long and painful period, taping my eyes open before going to sleep. I childishly hoped that this would reshape my eyes into a more open-shaped Western eye. I also developed a specific skin cleaning regime with carbolic soap, or coal tar soap if I couldn't find the carbolic. I would scrub, scrub, and scrub until my eczema-riddled skin was red and sometimes bleeding. I thought that this would eventually get rid of the "yellow" colored skin and I'd wake up one day, like Pinocchio, a real child; a white child with wide eyes and a bridge to my nose. We all know of course that that was never going to happen. My DIY solutions were not going to alter my physical appearance.

The only things that I got from these actions were a severe eye infection and further complications to my existing infantile eczema. My adoptive parents just ignored me and my attempts to change my appearance. Problems with my skin were put down to the eczema, the eye problems I developed were put down to the fact that I suffered from sties and sore eyes anyway. People only saw what they wanted to see. That meant ignoring the sticky tape marks on my eyes and the obvious red marks on my nose. That in turn meant that no one, including my adoptive parents, had to face any ugly questions. The questions no one wanted to be asked. It was easier to put your fingers in your ears, ignore it, and hope that it would all go away. Well, it didn't because I was there to stay. I was stuck with them and they with me. In a world in which the major driving socialization forces of race, ethnicity, and color were something that no one wanted to talk about. No one wanted to admit that being raised in a white privileged home with Western values and philosophy wasn't the answer and solution to everything. It couldn't give a non-white child roots or social status. It couldn't give me a sense of belonging or real identity. The society that I grew up in sought to bury who and what I really was. Where I had come from. They thought that burying the past and only focusing on the future would be the best way to give me a new life. Instead this split me culturally, socially, and racially, giving me a "schizophrenic" identity and self-view. It's taken the best part of thirty years for me to unravel.

To those who would say that color, race, and ethnicity don't matter when it comes to the adoption placement of a child, I would beg to differ. I am neither pro- nor anti-adoption. Each placement must be done on its own merit, taking into account individual circumstances. My lack of cultural, historical, and racial understanding—plus my inability to speak Chinese, disabled me socially and culturally. As with many disabilities, the effects are long-lasting and more often than not are permanent. Those who seek to adopt transracially must be willing to learn and teach themselves about racial politics and socialization in the countries and communities that they seek to raise these children. The parents need to be rock-steady and comfortable discussing and talking about issues that many in society today feel uncomfortable with, such as race, ethnicity, prejudice, and bias. Those prospective adopting parents have to always have in their minds that their desires as a parent are secondary to the needs and wants of their transracially adopted child. The parents have to have knowledge of their children's race, culture, and heritage so that they can help their child come to terms with who and where they have come from. They are going to have to walk more than a mile in someone else's shoes. It will feel alien and strange as they have to find ways of equipping their child with the tools that they need to deal with racism, and with possible social exclusion by other members of their own race and ethnicity. They will need to find strategies that their child can use to cope with institutionalized and structural racism. Parents have to be sensitive to representations of their child's race, or the language which is used and how that can be employed to undermine and undervalue minorities. All of these factors, if left unchecked, weave together to devalue, debase, and denigrate the minority, and in turn to negate and strip away any pride or self-worth that a minority has within the wider society.

We want our children to be healthy and whole, don't we? This should also include the mental wellbeing of our adoptive children, surely? Blocking out aspects of who and what we are, as we all know, only comes back to haunt us, causing problems later on in life. If we are to avoid these problems in the future generations of transracially adopted children then surely we need to dig deep. We need to ask the uncomfortable questions of the potential adopters. I would not like to see any transracially adopted child go through what I have been through. I would not want anyone to experience the isolation, despair, and mental confusion that I have battled my way through. I wouldn't want to see another child raised in a family with the attitude that "love and money" are enough. I would like to think that any family entering into such an adoption would not be so naive, ignorant, or lacking in human understanding. But sadly even now in the twenty-first century there are people who delude themselves that to transracially adopt with success "all you need is love and money." Believe me, love and money alone are not enough. Transracially adopted children look to the parents to be their mirror into their past. Perhaps if I had been brought up during a time where heritage and difference in culture had been accepted and valued, I wouldn't have gone through the mental turmoil that I did. If East Asians had not been perceived merely as caricatures and stereotypes to be ridiculed, then finding and being secure in my own skin would not have taken so long.

After all, parents are the portal that should guide children to their heritage. Parents are the ones that should link the child to both past, present and future.

* * *

Lucy Chau Lai-Tuen, stage name Lucy Sheen
—Made in Hong Kong, exported to the UK as a transracial adoptee in 1960s. A dyslexic actor, writer, filmmaker, who loves Dim sum, Yorkshire puddings and a nice cuppa cha! Lucy trained at the Rose Bruford College of Speech and drama and graduated in 1985. Her first professional job was the female lead in the ground breaking British-Chinese feature film, *Ping Pong* (1987). Her film credits include *Secrets & Lies, Something Good: The*

Mercury Factor. Her published writing includes *The Dance is New; Perpetual Child, An Adult Adoptee Anthology;* and *Adoptionland: From Orphan to Activist*. Lucy is currently developing several writing projects for stage and screen.

Chapter 9—Late Discovery Adoptees: The Original Victims of Identity Theft

By Lesli Maul, LCSW

> *I do not fit in.*
> *I do not belong.*
> *I have no place.*

had believed these things for as long as I can remember. They were the themes of my life. I did not have a happy, idyllic childhood. I grew up feeling disconnected and out of place, never really belonging with anyone or anywhere. There always seemed to be some factor that separated me and made me different. And at least in my eyes, the disparities I felt seemed obvious and loomed large. I was convinced that others could see how uncomfortable I always felt and easily identified me as someone with little value and not worth getting to know. This left me feeling isolated and alone; scared of letting others get to know me. I blamed it all on being an only child in a very small, dysfunctional family that liked to move frequently. What I did not know was that my family contained a secret. A secret that enveloped and obscured me. This secret was the fuel that my family ran on. It drove poor communication, substance abuse, depression, and emotional disconnection. Within me, it took the form of shame, destroying my self-worth and making it nearly impossible to feel safe in my own world. It has been a long journey of self-discovery and healing for me. It has taken almost five decades to find the place I fit. But I have found it, I am here now, and I am grateful. There are plenty of days I still want to go back and change the details of my life. I hate that I was lied to for so long, that I was not trusted to hold the truth of my existence, but I must move forward. Our strength is in our story, so I share mine and all the learning that has come thus far.

I am a late discovery adoptee. I grew up being told that I was the biological child of my parents. Learning of my adoption was surprising but not terribly shocking. I had always known something was not quite right. As I grew into and adjusted to the new knowledge that I was adopted at birth, my identity began to shift and I embarked on the telling of my story. I realized over time, however, that my course was different from those of other adult adoptees. I began to take note of the consistent startled reactions of others when I shared the details of my late discovery. Their genuine shock and disbelief that I had been deceived by my family seemed to make my reality increasingly painful. I noticed over time that I began to hide this part of my adoption narrative. I wanted to avoid the shame that was once again surfacing when I chronicled the dishonesty with which I was raised. As a seasoned therapist, you would think that I would have been familiar with the term late discovery adoptee, but I was not. The concept of "LDA" is something I stumbled upon two years ago while hunting around on the Internet. This concept has allowed me to journey through the second layer of shame that had begun to surface. Having a "real" name for my experience gave me access to information and a community. A community that completely understood what I experienced and how I felt. For the first time in my life I thoroughly fit somewhere. I was no longer alone or feeling the need to hide the unflattering details of my adoption story. It was the wrapping of specific terms and concepts around my experience that facilitated me emerging from the fog and moving towards the healing of my adopted self. I had no idea that feeling so disconnected and different from everyone up until this point had kept me so stuck. At last I had found the piece that allowed me to move forward with courage and authenticity.

My story is this: at age nineteen I was working my part-time job as a life guard at a community pool. I had the early bird shift that particular Monday morning in July. It was about 6:45 a.m., and I received a call from the front desk. A woman had come in and was asking to speak with me immediately. I remember being intrigued and thinking she probably had something pretty interesting to tell me as it was so early in the morning. I had no idea what was about to happen. So I had her sent back to the pool, and we sat down in the small glass office right off of the deck, where I could keep my eye on the swimmers that remained in the water.

I did not recognize the woman, but I noted that she seemed nervous. She was holding a small pile of papers and she stared at me quite intently. Her first statements to me were verifying my name, place of birth, and date of birth. Yes, she had all of my correct information. The next thing she said was, "Do you know you are adopted?" That is where the details become fuzzy for me and life as I knew it begins to spiral out of control. I do remember telling her, no, I was not aware that I was adopted, but that I had always secretly suspected it. In fact, at sixteen, I had shared this suspicion with my best friend, who then went on to ask my parents if it was true. I can still hear my father's stern, angry words to me that day, telling me that I was certainly *not adopted and I was never to question it again*! His tone and demeanor were so intimidating to me that I immediately blocked further thoughts of adoption from my awareness. That is, until that morning when the truth finally surfaced.

Back on the pool deck, this gentle woman showed me the documents she was holding, which confirmed everything she was telling me. At some point she also shared with me that she was my birth mother, but when and how I simply cannot recall. The rest of our time together, which was very short as she had to catch a plane, is a blur. I know that we took pictures and I made a quick phone call to some friends that lived nearby, asking them to come and witness what was happening in my life. I knew that I would need their support and confirmation that indeed my life had just irreversibly changed course. Then I said goodbye to this kind and beautiful stranger who was now my mother.

Three days later my birth father flew into town and asked to meet me. This time I was better prepared. My house phone rang one afternoon. I picked it up and a male voice inquired if I was Lesli. When I said, "Yes," he asked, "Do you know who this is?" I instinctively did. We met at a local A&W restaurant that afternoon and talked into the evening. It was an easy conversation, and I remember hanging on his every word. The emotional draw I felt towards both him and my birth mother was and is indescribable. It was such a relief to know that all of the unnamed anguish I had felt over the years had a real source. I was not the bad, ungrateful, or selfish person who I had come to believe I was. Rather, I had experienced a traumatic loss. It was a loss that eluded words, not only because it happened before I had the ability to think or speak, but also because I had been deliberately mislead for nineteen years. But now I knew the truth. I had been grieving all of my life and denied direct access to these feelings. I enjoyed my time with my birth father that day. We eventually said our goodbyes, and the next chapter of my journey immediately began.

The details of my reunion are not relevant for this chapter. What is important is, that for me having no knowledge of my adoption meant there was no childhood longing for the truth of my identity, no dream of the "ghost kingdom" to which I belonged, and no searching crowds for faces that looked like mine. Adoptees often have fantasies about their biological families. These fantasies contain personality traits, archetypes, and story lines that assist the adoptee in managing feelings of loss and abandonment. The term, "ghost kingdom," was aptly coined by Betty Jean Lifton (1979) to convey the elusive and haunting nature of the adoptee's drives and needs. I was spared these common adoptee experiences; instead, I, like most LDAs, had an ever-growing sense that things were "off." As LDAs, we are a small group. We are estimated to make up between nine- and eleven-percent of the adoptee population (Perl & Markman, 1999; Riley, 2013). Our stories are varied, but we are bound by the deception we were all raised under and the betrayal we subsequently experienced when we learned the truth. We are very familiar with "the bottom dropping out of our lives" feeling and know intimately the agonizing road to piecing our lives back together. We have each had to address loss, grief, forgiveness, identity redevelopment, and the restoration of balance and control in our lives. The duplicity with which we were raised leaves us uncertain about who to trust and how much to invest in others. Consequently, we have a great deal of difficulty allowing others into our worlds, revealing our genuine selves and forming healthy bonds. We instead frequently choose isolation over the risk of being hurt, rejected, or betrayed yet again. Much of this is also true for many aware adoptees. The difference for the LDA is the degree of awareness and betrayal. It becomes very easy for us all to fall into the self-protecting trap of avoiding true connection with others. Sadly that *never* leads to a full, healthy life.

Following my discovery, I spent the next year in a state of shock and crisis. I tried to make sense of everything, but all that I had known and believed was taken away. I was lost and tumbling into an abyss with no idea how to stabilize myself. One of the few clear memories I have of this time is receiving a phone call at work from a very nice lady. She identified herself as a representative of a local birth mother/adoptee support organization. She had been given my name by my birth mother and she wanted to reach out to me and let me know that support was available. I thanked her and took the information but never contacted her again. I was a teenager, barely on the cusp of adulthood, overwhelmed, with no idea what I needed or what would help. Looking back, I see this as one of those moments that I should have allowed the wisdom and support of someone else to help me. Those first few months post-discovery are so very tender. No one should have to go through them alone. I would have benefitted from someone to guide me through the crisis, reassure me that I would not always feel so lost, help me sort through my feelings, and assist me in understanding how to manage the paradoxical reactions of betrayal and loyalty I was experiencing.

With a simple conversation, my world was shattered and in the months that followed, the edges of my life became increasingly fuzzy, rolling up the sharp pieces of my broken identity and tucking them away so that I would not be destroyed. Then right on schedule, the fog rolled in. It limited my vision to only that which was directly in front of me, keeping "threatening" thoughts far from my mind, and moving me forward with only a partially formed sense of self. In spite of all this, I do realize that I am one of the lucky ones. The news of my adoption was given to me in a loving and gentle way (and for this I will be forever thankful). When the news is delivered in anger, spite, or because someone has been backed into a corner, it tends to be traumatic, furthering the pain in an already devastating situation. And yes, my world bottomed out in that moment of admission, but it was quickly replaced with a basic foundation of information about who I was and where I came from. I was able to avoid the distressing path of searching that many LDAs embark on. A path that for LDAs is almost as vital as breathing. Finding our birth families and working to recapture a sense of who we are through them is fundamental to our functioning.

Society is not always keen on search and reunion for adoptees, however. Adoptees are frequently viewed as ungrateful and disloyal should they embark on the natural quest for their families of origin. This is even truer for

LDAs. After all, our truth was buried and it was planned that we would never know the existence of our birth families. Stories of our entrance into the world were crafted for us to believe so that we would unwittingly collude in the "biological fantasy." Choosing to search is a pivotal point in healing for the LDA and not undertaken lightly. Embarking on a search frequently elicits anger and rejection from our adoptive families and even friends. It is rare for adoptive parents to transition into the supportive roles we need so much. Moving forward from this place of tangible distain is not easy for the LDA. But like most adoptees, LDAs have a natural curiosity about their birth families and a drive to fit in somewhere.

From an early age most of us know something is not right. My recollections of all the pieces not fitting together within my family begin at about age five. Many of us even suspect adoption throughout the years. However, like all other adoptees, we are keen observers of those around us and instinctively know what others need from us. We understand the nonverbal communication and unspoken family rules long before anyone else. Since a major driving force within our lives is to avoid being abandoned or rejected again, we quiet our concerns, silence our questions, and internalize everything as a way to cope. Our truth becomes the unspoken darkness and fear within us; the uneasiness we are not allowed to verbalize but must live with every day. This disquiet forms a barrier between the world and us. It keeps us numb, safe, and desperately disconnected.

The adoption fog is a state-of-mind the adoptee utilizes to keep going in the world. It is a coping technique that helps manage painful emotions. The fog tells us that our adoption has had no substantial impact on us and allows us reprieve from distressing feelings. The LDA differs slightly, in that we clearly acknowledge the negative impact of the deception we experienced, but the fog can obscure further investigation into how deeply our losses actually run. The fog helps us achieve milestones, reach goals, and sometimes just get through the day. With LDAs, the fog can help us maintain relationships as we sort through complicated reactions and emotions and begin to rebuild our identities. Understand, I am not saying that the fog is a good thing, only that it does have a role. The fog allowed me to get married, go to graduate school, give birth to two sons, and open my own therapy practice. The fog allowed me to push myself and not get distracted. I was able to accomplish all that I had set out to, without getting sidelined by pain or loss. I know that without the fog I might have gotten stuck in my development and feelings of inferiority, unable to give my all to my marriage, family, and career. So I pushed and I drove myself and I accomplished all that I had set out to do. For those reasons, I honor the fog as a part of my LDA process. I thank it for the opportunities it opened to me and the resilience it left me with. Peacefully, I have let it go once and for all.

Once we reach this point, as adoptees, we are able to look back with clarity. I now see what I could not before, even though it all seems so obvious. So what did the fog keep me from seeing and feeling? The first is my struggle with relationships and authenticity. When I finally emerged, I was able to look at my patterns in relationships and see how I hid from them and within them. My entire life I have had trouble letting go and being myself. I had firmly believed that others would simply not like me if they really knew me. So I watched for what others needed me to be, became that person, and then scrutinized all encounters I had with others for evidence that I had done or said something wrong. I recognize that these social acrobatics are very much an adoptee trait, but I also believe that they develop from the LDA's early sense that something is "off" within the family. What results from these primal, invalidated suspicions is an internalized sense of wrongness. LDAs do not trust themselves to know how to act or what to say, so they look externally for clues. For so many years of my life I worked very hard to stay just under the radar, moving forward quietly, and trying not to call too much attention to myself or upset anyone, lest someone see the inquietude I felt.

This very quickly segues into the second negative aspect of the fog: the inability to see our intense and irrational fear of rejection and abandonment. I was so terrified of being rejected that my default behavior became silence. I lost my voice in most situations. It was easier to say nothing than to risk saying something wrong and experiencing disapproval. All of my life, I preferred loneliness to being disliked or left out. The evidence of this came in my sophomore year of college. My family was going through some major shifts and my adoptive parents decided to move back to the States. I wanted to remain in Canada (where we had moved when I was thirteen), so I transitioned into my university's dorms.

This happened just two months after learning of my adoption. I immediately began to struggle more socially. It became almost incapacitating. I avoided dorm group activities and the dining hall. I even got to the point where I was skipping most of my classes. My abandonment was triggered with my adoptive parents leaving, and the fear of not fitting in with the other dorm residents became something to avoid at all costs. At the end of the year there was a dorm banquet. The few people that I did know talked me into going. During the awards segment of the banquet, I received the "Ghost of the Year" award. Although it was meant in jest, it called attention to my overwhelming pain and ineffective attempts to manage it. The award culminated a sorrow-filled year for me and served to intensify my decades-long avoidance patterns. At the time, I did not recognize the degree of emotional distress I was going through. I had no clue how to help myself and not further my isolation. This was another interchange of my life where therapy and specific support could have proven invaluable.

The fog also kept me from genuinely grieving all that I had lost for a very long time. LDAs must face a multitude of losses, including that of their birth mother, their identity and history, and the ability to trust those around them. The fog can act as a buffer for the staggering amount of adjustment that is required of LDAs once we learn the truth, allowing us to take it a little at a time. It is typically a life event that becomes the catalyst for fully emerging from the fog, such as getting married, becoming pregnant, or assuming parenthood. As the fog completely lifts, we are faced with powerful emotions that require our attention and patience. It is in the processing of this grief that some amazing wisdom can develop. For example, it was only in grieving the loss of my birth mother that I realized my own importance to my two sons. It facilitated an even stronger connection and understanding of my role in their lives. It also helped me to develop the resiliency I needed to get through the tough parenting times, mastering the awareness that our bond was deeper than whatever transient struggle we were experiencing. To me, the gift of my motherhood has been the greatest treasure of the fog lifting.

Finally, once the fog lifts we are able to address the betrayal that has caused us to have the moniker, "Late Discovery Adoptee" in the first place. For me, it took over two decades to speak the truth to my adoptive parents. Of this I am not proud; and most LDAs do not wait that long. But for me, I understood the negative, angry, and rejecting reaction I was likely to face from my adoptive parents, and I simply could not do it. For a long time I pretended my fictitious existence was "no big deal." On the other side of my reality, I was trying to cope with complicated reunions, filled with more than my share of disappointment and heartbreak. I was just not ready to deal with it from all sides. For many years I lived in three separate worlds—that of my adoptive parents, that of my maternal birth family, and that of my paternal birth family. I was forced to compartmentalize these three sectors of my life, understanding that none of the families had any interest in knowing of the others. This situation caused me to feel fragmented a great deal of the time, much like a child of divorce. So, I took the route of least resistance with my adoptive family and allowed their veil of denial regarding my adoption to continue.

What finally prompted me to speak the truth and honor my life for exactly what it was, was the untimely death of my paternal brother. We had enjoyed a sibling relationship for seventeen years, and when he died, the last bit of my fog evaporated. Facing this direct loss of someone I deeply loved caused me to see the relevance of not only his life, but mine as well. I deserved to live authentically and with integrity. So I shared with my adoptive parents what I knew, including the fact that I had just lost a close sibling. The reaction was exactly what I had anticipated: anger, defensiveness, and an attempt to shift the blame to me. Through my work in therapy and as a therapist, I was able to set boundaries, express myself clearly, and remain firm in my truth. My adoptive parents have never spoken of my adoption or the loss of my brother again, and our relationship remains as it has always been, superficial and limited. To my delight, however, the fog is gone and I feel much happier. The shame I have carried around all of my life has departed and I now live with more courage and authenticity than I ever thought possible. I no longer work to stay invisible in my own life but instead embrace challenges and take risks. I share more of myself with others and accept that rejection and failure may be the result.

Moving forward following discovery, what does an LDA need? First and foremost we need recognition and validation. We need our adoptive families to own their duplicitous behaviors and offer us honesty. We need an apology for the chronic, unexplainable ache we have had to live with our entire lives and verification that this pain has been real for us. We do not expect anyone to understand what it feels like to be us, but we need to know we do not have to continue to face our losses alone. We need others to recognize that our losses exist.

We need understanding and support as we slowly try to pull the fragments of our lives back together into something familiar and yet unmistakably different. Nothing makes sense to us for quite a while, and most LDAs are working to rebuild their world from the ground up. Because discovery of adoption can be traumatic, many LDAs find returning to their lives quite challenging. Resuming established roles (e.g. student, parent, spouse, employee) may seem almost impossible, and we may even have a period of acting out our frustrations. With time and patience, new ways of being are learned and incorporated. We need those around us to respond with empathy and compassion, so that we can learn self-compassion, a skill most often underdeveloped in LDAs.

As LDAs, we need the freedom to search. Since everything feels lost to us, we are drawn back to the beginning, the place where we began, and to the people we originated from. We need a story and family to which we can tether our burgeoning identities. Our motives, loyalties and, judgment are often called into question when we finally do decide to search. Without support from those in our circles, shame and guilt flourish, often leading us to cease the search, at least until adoptive parents have died. Or, we continue our search in secret. None of these options are ideal for our healing. We need the freedom to search openly, and should reunion become a reality, we need acceptance of our interest to pursue relationships with our birth families. Since so much of our lives have already been lived in silence, allowing us to share our ongoing stories openly is the greatest gift we can receive.

Our drive to search is our way of restoring a healthy sense of control and power back in our lives. Our stories have been taken from us. We are the original victims of identity theft. We have experienced the triple jeopardy of loss; of our first families, of our identities, and of our ability to trust others freely and without question. It is us alone that can begin to restore our sense of "rightness" in the world, and each of us will go about this in our own way. For some it may be unplugging from adoptive families and friends for a while, for others it may involve moving away and starting a fresh life, some may change jobs, write a book, go back to school or become involved in an adoptees' rights organization. Whatever form it takes for us, understand we are trying to reorient ourselves. For the first time we are making decisions based on our truth.

The road to wholeness for the LDA is by no means easy. It is tumultuous, confusing, and at times just as devastating as when the news was first learned. My story continues to unfold before me. Sometimes I am active in making things happen and others times things shift for me without my direct involvement, even after twenty-nine years. I have learned to accept the distant relationship with my adoptive parents, and I have become well acquainted with the various stages of reunion. I no longer organize my life around the beliefs that I have little value to others, and that I do not matter as a human being. I have learned to embrace my story as an LDA and find my strength within it. Being found and reuniting with both sides of my birth family has left me both exhilarated and distraught. I have no idea how those relationships will ultimately turn out—I hope well—but at this point, I believe in my resiliency above all else. I do continue to feel like somewhat of a misfit, but I have learned to honor that as my uniqueness. In fact, there is somewhere that I fit perfectly, a safe place I go to for refuge and to refuel. That place is with my circle of support, my husband, my two sons, my small group of close family and friends and at long last, my cohort of other late discovery adoptees. They all know my story and offer me the unconditional love and acceptance I have been seeking most of my life. No one in this circle asks me to change or shift to please him or her. It is here that I belong.

References

Lifton, Betty Jean. *Lost and Found: The Adoption Experience* (New York: Dial, 1979).

Perl. L. and S. Markham. *Why wasn't I told? Making sense of the late discovery of adoption* (Paddington, NSW: The Benevolent Society of New South Wales, 1999).

Riley, D. H. "Confronting the conspiracy of silence and denial of difference for late discovery adoptive persons and donor conceived people" in *Australian Journal of Adoption*, 7(2), 2013.

* * *

Lesli Maul, LCSW is a licensed clinical social worker whose career spans two and a half decades. The past twelve have been in private practice. She enjoys speaking to groups about courage, authenticity, and wholehearted living. Each October she offers a workshop to adoptees entitled, "The Daring Way™ for Adult Adoptees: Our Strength is in Our Stories." Currently she is working on certification in Animal Assisted Psychotherapy.

She is a Baby Scoop Era adoptee in reunion. She lives in Southern California with her husband and two sons. Other passions include her rescue animals (two dogs and one cat), gardening and quilting.

Chapter 10—Adoptees and Intimacy: Of Fear, Yearning, and Restoring the Capacity for Connection

By Karen Caffrey, LPC, JD and Jodi Haywood

Jodi—Creating closeness. It seems to come more naturally to some people than others, even other adoptees. Growing up in an international adoption with relatives I hadn't met until they took me to live with them at twenty-one-months-old, I avoided getting close to people, particularly the adopters. I wanted friends, people to hang out with so that I didn't have to spend so much time at "home," but I wasn't sure how to "do" relationships, or even if I wanted to. That would mean getting close to people. With the adopters being my third set of caregivers, who in turn left me with other caregivers during the day, along with some vague memories of abuse that still wake me up in the middle of the night—the last thing I wanted was closeness, physical or emotional, with another human being.

Add to this the fact I felt betrayed by the adopters, after they admitted at the end of my seventh grade year that one of them was my biological aunt. From this I deduced they hadn't even wanted to take me in; I was an abandoned relative she'd saved from being raised in an orphanage. People could not be trusted.

Once in a while over my life, someone has managed to work their way past several of my barriers into a semblance of closeness. This requires a lot of effort on their part and is not an easy task to undertake. But occasionally it happens.

In the last year, I've done a huge amount of healing from adoption trauma, to the point of returning to college in order to become a therapist for post-adoption issues and attachment problems. My biggest question to myself when Karen and I set out to write this chapter was: "Why do I even want to create closeness? It's so much easier to maintain a safe distance." Well, maybe it is, but unless you're ready to leave it all behind and go become a hermit somewhere beyond the fringes of civilization, you're likely to engage in some level of human contact. If you're adopted and curious about it, you're likely to search for your original family. It's also possible that some of them will search for you.

Nearly every religion, philosophy, and belief system includes the concept that we humans are social creatures. We grow up in families (some less functional than others), we attend school, we work in offices or trades or stores. Even working from home involves some interaction with others. And the prevailing view among society is: if you're antisocial, there's something "wrong" with you. Even if there isn't, a complete lack of socialization can *result* in serious mental and/or emotional problems.

I wasn't raised in a Christian home, but I have been active in various churches since I was fifteen. Since I began writing my part of this project, I've heard several times from a variety of sources—some friends, some random acquaintances who know nothing of my subject matter – that "God created us for relationship." I have heard it so many times in so many forms, I'm not even sure who to attribute the original quote to. Whether I like it or not, feel comfortable with it or not, if I'm going to exist as part of God's creation (whatever your perception may be of the creative being), He is going to bring relationships into my life. The better developed my "closeness skills" are, the easier those relationships will be to handle. We're meant to be companions to one another on the healing journey, sometimes helping a traveler along by sharing our knowledge and survival tips, and sometimes being the one in need.

It's especially important to work on your capacity for closeness when you have a family of your own. I see my relationships with my husband and daughter as lifelong. Part of my reason for wanting to get married was my desire to choose who I belonged to: someone other than the adopters, whom I did not choose. Getting rid of their name by replacing it with that of the man who loved me, who chose me as his other half. Forsaking all others sounded good to me. We've held it together for fifteen years now, because I decided I wanted closeness with this man, and nothing and no one would come between us. Sometimes it's hard to make the choice to spend time with somebody when you'd rather be alone, to connect when your first impulse is to withdraw, to believe him when he says he loves you. Sometimes the hardest thing to believe about love is that it won't abandon you. Many of us adoptees have had it drilled into us that our mothers loved us enough to give us away, leading us to assume that the most loving thing somebody can do for us is to abandon us to complete strangers. I didn't realize the full impact of growing up without a mom - without the mother-daughter bond - until the birth of my own daughter left me clueless. How could I forge a bond with her when I had no prior experience? How could I mother when I had never truly been mothered? We need to rewire our thought patterns and impulses to handle this new programming, and it can be a lifelong challenge.

So I'm here partly as an adoptee and partly as a counselor in training who needs to know how to build close—and healthy—relationships in order to help others develop those skills.

Karen—In this eloquent introduction Jodi reveals several challenges to intimacy that she personally faces, which are also common among adoptees. These challenges can be especially strong in adoptees who, like Jodi, have had more than one disruption in their early primary attachments. The very first challenge, of course, is answering, "Why bother getting close to people?" The tragedy of this question is that only someone who has found relationships to be more trouble than they are worth would ask it. It is indeed a tragedy when the very thing that is supposed to provide us comfort, support, ease, and joy brings pain and emptiness instead.

The good news is that Jodi has figured out that there must be some reason so many people think having close relationships is a good idea. Even better, her faith/belief system supports this premise. I see this as a big positive, since someone who truly does not believe that close relationships hold any value for them will not try to create them. In my experience it is unlikely that such a person would seek either psychotherapy or the kind of close personal relationship that has the ability to heal and transform. Therapy is designed to create a relationship between the client and therapist as a vehicle for growth, and often has an explicit goal of helping the client learn how to create closer relationships with others. If someone is not willing to take the risk of getting close to anyone at all, creating closeness is going to be extremely difficult or impossible. Intention, as always, steers the ship. And Jodi's intention is to be able to get closer to people.

Another common challenge Jodi is facing is the fear of abandonment, which is practically ubiquitous among adoptees. There is a mistaken belief in the adoptee's developmentally younger mind that "I *will be* left," which is based on the child's actual experience that "I *was* left." The danger is when the adoptee projects this belief into the present and believes or fears it is the truth *now*. This is an intimacy-crippling belief that prevents the adoptee from allowing herself to become close to anyone in the present, lest she re-experience the old pain of abandonment. Paradoxically, it is the present day experience of "I am here with you *now*" that heals the old abandonment trauma.

No degree of presence on the part of a therapist or any other person will fully heal the adoptee until they untangle the old abandonment fear/projection. Because the adoptee will always be able to say, "You just haven't left me *yet*. You might die/change your mind/stop loving me." Since this a factual possibility, the adoptee can always hold back a piece of her from the relationship, thereby holding back a piece of her from healing.

The truth is that an adult can be left by another person and the adult will (eventually) be okay. Adults don't abandon themselves. They know they can take care of themselves, survive, live on to love another day, etc. Only in the younger, child mind place is abandonment experienced as a "forever trauma." Healing this young place of abandonment opens the door to the richness of deep intimacy, a relationship capacity for which we are naturally wired.

Healing from our first abandonments, accepting our truth

Jodi—Adoption goes against nature. Naturally, my adopter was my aunt; however I don't believe she had the right to interfere with that biological relationship with my mother. Adopting me, particularly the way she went about it, infringed not only on my right as a human being, but on my mother's right to leave me in what she believed was a safe temporary environment with my paternal grandparents. Adopting me betrayed my mother's trust in my father's side of the family, because she intended to come back for me and was not given the opportunity to do so. I realize that the term "adopter" does dehumanize her, but when I discovered at age twelve that she was my biological aunt and wanted to call her that—since I had no other aunts or uncles by blood—she snapped at me as if I'd overstepped her boundaries.

Mostly I do refer to her as my aunt, or my aunt adopter, which defines the relationship. Neither of my parents actually gave me up for adoption; in fact, both of them fought it, separately. I have this mental image of this adopter-puppeteer pulling the strings and orchestrating everybody's life according to her will. I wasn't able to cut the strings at the time, only stretch them to the fullest possible extent. She would have slapped or shamed me for calling her "aunt" during her lifetime, but now that she's dead, I'm free to define the relationship in my own terms. As for my uncle, I've called him by his first name for as long as I can remember. I already had a daddy, and while his sister did her best to keep me away from him, she couldn't change the blood relationship or my feelings for him.

Karen—While at first blush it might seem like Jodi's experience is unique in that her "relinquishment" by her birth parents was not truly voluntarily, in fact this is far more commonly the case than most people are aware. Jodi is unique in that she possesses more truth about her personal history than many adoptees, so she knows this truth.

The historical reality is that many and perhaps the majority of birth mothers experienced forced relinquishments as a result of societal and familial shaming. Many women still face pressures by the for-profit adoption industry which results in them choosing a "permanent solution to a temporary problem." (viz.— relinquishing their child to adoption when, with adequate support, they could parent their child either immediately or in the near future).

Many adoptees have a multitude of feelings about being "given away" or abandoned by their biological mother: anger, betrayal, hurt, etc. At some point they may learn either through education (viz.—reading Ann Fessler's *The Girls Who Went Away*), their adoption files, or their actual birth mother that the truth is considerably more complicated. This is particularly challenging when facts discovered later in life, like in Jodi's situation, don't mesh with the information with which she was raised.

I also want to note that Jodi is probably not being politically correct when she says "Adoption is against nature." (We could write a whole book about that statement alone!) I support her in claiming her own truth and her own language, as she also does when she refers to her adoptive mother/aunt as her aunt, or aunt adopter. Healing isn't about being politically correct. It is about finding and expressing our truth, and if necessary amending that truth along the way. We can't be close to someone to the extent we are hiding our true selves by being "nice."

Adoption language and adoptee behavior

Jodi—There's nothing politically correct about honest adoption dialogue, nor should there be, if honesty is to be encouraged. Historically, the goal of post-adoption therapy (when addressed at all) is to integrate the adopted child into his or her new family, regardless of differences in background, race, ethnicity, culture, etc. Adoptees are generally viewed as healthy, well-adjusted and successful when they behave "as if born to"—compliant, obedient, making every effort to fit in with the adoptive family while seldom or never, speaking of their biological family or raising questions about their origins. On the other hand, adoptees who "act out" are berated for doing so—punished for their attempts to resist adapting and assert their own independence, and considered ungrateful when they dare to acknowledge the fact they have another family to whom they are blood-related and desire to know more about that family, even to know their own family. This behavior is too often perceived as a disorder that must be altered, rather than the sign of a wound in desperate need of healing.

I think that for older adoptees, with stronger attachments to the original parent(s) or possibly other caregivers, there is more of a tendency to "act out." Some experts say this is our way of testing the new family, pushing the limits, trying to see how much we can get away with and still be kept. Rejection resulting from these behaviors only reinforces our feeling of being unwanted. Another possibility, which doesn't seem to have been mentioned much in what I've read, is a genuine desire on the part of the adoptee to be sent "back home" or to another family. If the compliant adoptee is afraid to speak out for fear of being sent away, the rebellious one may feel a sense of entrapment. Frequent episodes of running away or getting "lost" can be a manifestation of this desire.

I remember several such episodes from my own childhood. Wandering away from my adopting aunt and visiting grandmother in a crowded department store, taking the time to look at everything I wanted to see, enjoying the freedom I felt at escaping their hold. I was in no hurry to see them again, even as they frantically searched the store for me. I was disappointed when a policeman apprehended me, maybe two hours later, and returned me to them. Another time, my adopting uncle took me to a county fair and the same thing happened: I got distracted by something, and next thing I knew, I'd lost him. I had a great time exploring the midway on my own until someone took me to the lost children's tent, where I gave the officials a false name. You might have called me a free-spirited kid with a vivid imagination, but the truth was I longed for the home I'd once known and the family that did not include this couple who'd adopted me. I never considered it fair that the adoption contract, which changed my whole life and cut me off from my own parents, required no consent on my part.

Karen—It is no small thing that Jodi points out she had no consent (and no voice) when she was the object of a legal contract that permanently changed her life. It is beyond many people's ability to comprehend that being adopted means someone legally took possession of your body, changed your name, and deprived you of your ancestry without your consent. (If you really try this on emotionally you will probably find yourself slipping towards a feeling of horror.) What impact might it have on your ability to trust and be close to people when you have been treated thus when you were completely vulnerable? It has happened to every adoptee.

Jodi is also once again giving voice to a truth that she may have more access to than many adoptees, that truth being that she had a home and identity before she was adopted. Historically, acknowledging this truth was the cardinal sin in the adoptive family as well as among adoption professionals. Good, well-adjusted adoptees pretended, along with their adoptive families, that they simply did not exist prior to joining the adoptive family.

Closeness is a function of sharing our deepest selves with another. Pretending that a part of our identity does not exist, or that it isn't important, creates a barrier to self-knowledge and thus to one's capacity for intimacy. I can't share with *you* what I don't have of *me*. Piercing the myth of the adoptee's non-existence prior to adoption, and coming to grips with whatever factual information may be available to an adoptee, can only augment the capacity for closeness.

The two common adaptive behaviors/defenses Jodi discusses above (compliance and acting out) were first described in Nancy Verrier's groundbreaking book, *The Primal Wound*. I highly recommend it to anyone who wishes to understand the experience of being adopted. As we are illuminating here, both of these behaviors have negative consequences for the capacity for intimacy.

Jodi—The first set of behaviors (which can manifest on a spectrum, with some adoptees being far more compliant and submissive than others), gives the impression of closeness while concealing any thoughts or emotions contradictory to the idea that the adoptive home is the happiest of all possible worlds. In at least some cases, compliance is a façade created so as not to cause disharmony in the adoptive family.

The compliant adoptee can easily become a people-pleaser with no real sense of her own self, her own needs or desires, or how to meet those needs—while being an expert at meeting the needs of others. Ignoring or concealing one's own needs results in the lack of vulnerability required for genuine closeness. Others may draw close because they see someone who can help them meet their own needs, but eventually leave once those needs are met, or be driven away out of frustration because a real give-and-take relationship is not possible.

The second behavioral spectrum, while not conducive to creating closeness in the adoptive family, may be much closer to the adoptee's true struggle: between trusting and isolating oneself, between belonging and feeling like an outcast or misfit, between risking closeness and keeping people at a safe distance. These people may have a stronger awareness of adoption issues and the effects of these issues on their relationships, yet may be reluctant to attempt changing their behavior to encourage a deeper closeness.

This "acting out" behavior uses anger to push people away and maintain distance, although the anger itself may be a sign of vulnerability, because their real feelings can only be expressed when angry. There is a difference between healthy anger as a stage of grief or an indication that something is wrong, and ongoing, uncontrollable rage; it's important to know the difference.

Overcoming the "as if" mentality and understanding the effects of adoption trauma

Karen—I suspect therapists are less likely to see adoptees in therapy for adoptee-related issues if they are caught up in the "as if born to this family" paradigm. Adoptees in the "as if" state of mind are not likely to allow themselves to perceive any need for their birth identity or origins, since they would consider such a need to be disloyal to their adoptive parents and family. This may be particularly true for older adoptees who were raised when then "as if" paradigm reigned supreme.

In recent years both society and adoption professionals adhere less strongly to the "as if" mentality and acknowledge to at least some extent the importance of birth origins. Nevertheless these adoptees may come to therapy for any of the many other issues that everyone else comes to therapy: anxiety, depression, relationship issues, etc.

We therapists should hold an awareness of the potential impact of being adopted for these clients, just as we hold other information about the client in our awareness even if the client is not yet ready to consider it. The work then must address when and how to assist the adoptee in bringing awareness to their collusion in the "as if" belief system, and the impact it may be having on their capacity for closeness.

An adoptee in "acting out" mode may come to therapy believing that it is **true** that they don't belong or fit in. They also may believe that it is **safe** to keep people at a distance. In fact, it is only safe to keep *unsafe* people at a distance. True safety is having the ability to distinguish safe people from unsafe people, and to protect oneself from the former while allowing closeness with the latter. An adoptee stuck in their child mind will (usually unconsciously) globalize the experience of lack of safety from their childhood to people in the present.

The work, however one approaches it, is about helping the adoptee distinguish between the child-mind sense of "not belonging"/lack of safety in the adoptive family, and the adult mind. In the present, an adult mind knows it is safe to belong deeply and fully to oneself and others in adult relationships. Like all beliefs developed in childhood, however, its hold can be tenacious.

I want to issue a caution here that we be very careful not to pathologize adoptees for having developed these defenses. Developing defenses to an overwhelming traumatic experience is a much needed survival mechanism. The historical refusal of society and the mental health system to acknowledge the trauma of being adopted has alienated many adoptees from resources that have the capacity to help and heal them. We don't tell a rape victim she is frigid. We help her recover from the trauma of sexual assault and regain her capacity for sexual experience. It is, sadly, an apt analogy for the mental health system's treatment of adoption trauma.

Jodi—The limited understanding of adoption trauma by society and most mental health practitioners often means that adoptees are discouraged from expressing their grief in healthy ways and moving through the stages of grieving. Adoptive parents may not realize the impact of significant loss on a young child's psyche; they may believe the child can "outgrow" it as quickly and easily as he or she outgrew baby clothes; they may view the child as overly sensitive and counter it with controlling, disciplinary action to the point of abuse; some feel helpless in the face of such deep grief and do not know how to handle it; and others fear the image of the child's healed, independent self, no longer needy, perhaps determined to seek out the natural parents or other biological connections.

Karen—As Jodi points out, grief over the many losses inherent in being adopted (of one's birth mother, birth father, birth-self, ancestral history, medical and genetic background, etc.) are treated as non-existent in the "as if born to this family" paradigm. Yet these losses are inherent to being adopted.

All parents and families have different capacities to tolerate and experience grief. An adoptee growing up in a grief-denying or grief-judging family will face significant challenges in both acknowledging the feelings behind their real losses and working through the inevitable related grief.

Jodi—There was no acknowledgment of grief in my adopters' home. I believe much of the reason behind this was the fact my aunt took me first and then began adoption proceedings, rather than receiving a child who had already been relinquished by her natural parents. She had to have some understanding that her actions were ethically and legally wrong, although I never saw any manifestation of guilt feelings. To accept my feelings of grief and loss, she would have had to accept her own responsibility as the one who caused me that loss. It's like a murderer facing the child she orphaned and admitting the consequences of her actions.

I have the files from the psychiatrists and other specialists my aunt took me to as a small child. After hearing about some of my early family disruption (much more information than I had at the time, although nowhere near the whole story), one psychiatrist suggested that my emotional and social difficulties might stem from these family problems and the trauma of being separated from my previous caregivers. My aunt refused to believe him and insisted that it all came from my "visual limitations" (I was born with very little sight in my left eye). It makes me wonder what scapegoat she might have used for a child with normal vision.

Karen—Jodi's situation is one where her losses were strongly denied, which of course prevented their resolution. For adoptees, there is (at least) a two-fold process of regarding adoption-related losses. The first is simply awareness and recognition of the losses themselves. (viz.—"I have no picture of myself as an infant." "I wasn't breast fed." "I don't know what my biological parents, or any other biological relative, looks like." "I don't resemble anyone I know.") The second is allowing the emergence whatever feelings arise with awareness of these losses, in particular the feeling of grief.

One of the deepest human experiences of closeness is the experience of grieving for a loss and being comforted by someone we experience as safe and loving. There are two separate aspects of comfort. The first is the behavior of the person doing the comforting, and the second is the subjective experience of the person who is being offered the comfort. That is, first, someone offers comfort (or occasionally their mere presence constitutes an offer of comfort). Second, the person who is distressed experiences their distress as being eased or alleviated. Being comforted is what happens when both of these are present. The experience of being comforted typically has both physical and emotional components. People who are feeling comforted may notice their muscles relax, their breathing slows, their mind stops racing, and their emotional pain dissipates.

If we have experienced significant losses and our grief about those losses is ignored and uncomforted (because the losses themselves cannot be acknowledged), our ability to be close to others is diminished.

Jodi—That's true. I have little or no memory of being comforted as a small child. My aunt would take care of me if I was sick, but my emotional needs went unmet. I actually can't remember specific times of feeling sad or lonely, maybe because that was a permanent state-of-being during my childhood. The sadness might be more intense, more profound, at some times than others, but it never really went away. I spent several years in one particular daycare, and the woman in charge threatened to punish me for crying—until I taught myself to hold it in.

I would say I never learned how to be comforted, or how to accept comforting. I have this friend, an older lady I consider my "spiritual mother." I first met her when I got sent to her for counseling; I was thirteen. At the end of our introductory meeting, after I'd rambled on for an hour about my parents and the adopters and all the ways my life had gone wrong, she wouldn't let me leave without a hug. I didn't know how to receive it. I just stood there with my arms hanging at my sides, fighting back tears, because if I started crying I wouldn't be able to stop. It took a long time, well over a year, before I could bring myself to return a hug from her. I'm glad she didn't give up on me. Looking back I realize how traumatized I must have been, the lack of trust that left me unable to respond to being comforted or loved.

I think it's difficult for adoptees to receive comfort. When we experience separation from our mothers at a very young age, it causes our anxiety levels to escalate, and when Mom doesn't come back, we develop many forms of self-soothing behaviors to try and calm that anxiety, or at least, override it in order to function. We simply aren't wired to seek that comfort from other people; we turn our need inward and look to sources we're able to control. Add to this the lack of trust and/or fear of abandonment we've discussed earlier and it's no wonder our "comfort receptors" don't work normally. Even when we encounter that rare person who cares enough to stand by us and tries to get through to us, we don't know how to reach out and ask them for the comfort we need. And sometimes the process of connecting with someone is the catalyst that brings our need for comfort to the surface. There may not be an external event that triggers it, like a loss or a major life change; only the added presence of someone who understands more than someone we've experienced previously. That connection in itself can be a major life change for us.

This is where people who become close to adoptees, either in a personal or professional setting, need to be aware of the repercussions of empathy. You may well be the first person from whom an adoptee has received unconditional love and acceptance. They'll soak it up like parched ground. This can put a strain on the relationship, especially when the counselor or friend isn't prepared for it: the adoptee may react with angry outbursts, cool aloofness, or childlike dependence, or all of the above and more. It's part of the grieving process, and as Karen has said, allowing comfort during grief is what builds our closest emotional connection with another human being. When you've lived your entire life—or your entire adopted life—in a state of alienation and emotional isolation, to suddenly experience this depth of connection means navigating new and foreign territory.

For the friend, counselor, or other professional, this can be a complicated situation to handle. Withdrawing comfort during the grieving process, without providing adequate coping skills, is detrimental and often devastating to the adoptee. It's like opening a deep wound and allowing it to bleed freely, then abandoning the patient. The wound needs to be sewn up or bandaged in order to complete the healing process. If it requires more time, skill, or attention than you are capable of giving, the patient—the adoptee—needs to understand that she is not being abandoned or relinquished to another caregiver. Until the adoptee develops adult coping skills, it is the "child mind" that Karen mentioned earlier with which she responds to abandonment, loss, or change in caregivers. The ideal scenario is for one constant person to walk the adoptee through the healing journey, although others may come alongside at various stages.

Some may disagree with my statement about "the first person from whom an adoptee has received unconditional love and acceptance." Keep in mind that giving and receiving are two different things. A well-meaning adoptive family can offer these gifts to a child, who may be too traumatized to recognize or receive them. A young child who has suffered abandonment by, or forced removal from, her family of origin has no concept of unconditional acceptance. A child raised in an abusive or dysfunctional adoptive home, where emotional neglect is more prevalent than comfort and where "love" is conditional upon performance, is not in a place to learn about healthy emotional connections.

Accepting comfort includes allowing ourselves to relax, let down our guard, take off our masks, becoming vulnerable. The adoption trauma "package" usually includes hyper vigilance, anxiety issues (including PTSD), and the fight-or-flight response. Relaxation tends to be a foreign concept to us: we can't relax if we don't feel safe, and vulnerability is the most unsafe thing we can be. Yet it is necessary to move beyond our safe zone, to work through every stage of our grief, in order to move forward to the point of acceptance—not necessarily accepting the adoptive family with open arms, but accepting the fact that the adoption occurred and the responsibility to come to terms with it.

Coming to terms with our adoption

Karen—I very much agree with Jodi's comments on the physiological correlation between relaxation and receiving comfort. Healing techniques that directly work with the body, both psychotherapeutic and otherwise (yoga, bodywork, tai chi, etc.) are essential to developing the capacity to receive comfort.

I also think Jodi sums up the healing process nicely when she says that moving forward involves "accepting the fact that the adoption occurred and the responsibility to come to terms with it." I agree with her qualification that this is "not necessarily accepting the adoptive family with open arms," at least to the extent that implies some sort of blind obedience or "drinking the Kool-Aid." All adults, whether adoptees or not, have the option of deciding what part of their family of origin they accept and what part they do not. And they have the choice about how to live that decision. Adult adoptees have a choice about whether and how to accept their adoptive families, and/or their beliefs about adoption or anything else.

Jodi—I didn't accept mine. I think acceptance and trust go hand-in-hand, and both take time to develop. Past experience has a lot of bearing on the length of time needed and the level of acceptance. Being taken just before the age of two, in an international adoption, having already endured some family upheaval, gives me a different perspective than someone adopted at birth into a more stable home. My mother had suffered domestic violence; my father went to jail, and I'd just lost my grandfather prior to being rehomed. That's a lot for an almost-two-year-old to go through. My aunt and uncle might not have handled me in a manner that inspired me to trust them. I probably wasn't ready to accept another drastic change in my living situation. And people aren't always a good fit for one another. We've heard so many recent stories in the news about couples adopting children, usually older children from other countries, and realizing they aren't equipped to handle them. I would say it's a lack of acceptance, on both sides. The children are old enough to know they don't want to be adopted, they don't want to belong to these new adults, and the adults don't know how to be what the children need. I think they desire so badly to be parents that they blind themselves to the fact the children do not want them as parents.

The manner in which adoptive parents handle the developing child's adopted status can be the biggest influence on creating closeness or distance. Are they honest about the adoption, the fact that the child was born to another mother? Do they encourage discussion and differences of opinion—not only pertaining to the adoption, but in ways that acknowledge the adopted child as an individual, rather than an extension of the adoptive parents? Do they encourage age-appropriate steps of independence, or restrain the adoptee in a state of perpetual childhood, perhaps out of fear that "their" child will seek reunion with the natural family? Excessive closeness, or smothering, often results in physical as well as emotional distance.

Karen—What Jodi is bringing to light here is the considerable importance of the psychology of the adoptive parent, who in her case was her aunt as well. What was her aunt thinking, and what were her motivations in taking Jodi? How would this impact her ability to be present to Jodi's feelings about adoption (or anything else for that matter)?

It can be very helpful to explore with the adoptee what they know about their adoptive parent's attitudes, beliefs, and experiences about adoption. Were they unable to have their own biological children, and did they grieve this loss? Do they view themselves as "rescuers" of unfortunate orphans or bastards? Was there any sense that one adoptive parent felt forced or coerced by the other, or by the expectations of the extended family to have children? And how would all of this impact the ability of the adoptive parent to support and parent the adoptee in addressing her experience of being adopted?

Jodi—This may be one of the things that sets a pattern of inconsistent, on-again-off-again relationships for adoptees. The adoptive parents are able to create a certain degree of closeness, wanting to be "good" parents, to be there for the child in every way—yet they cannot bring themselves to deal with the level of grief the adopted child has suffered and continues to suffer, because of the role they played in it. An adoptive mother may unconsciously distance herself from a daughter's sense of loss because she feels responsible for it, while the daughter places the burden of that rift upon herself and reaches the conclusion that nobody cares about, or wants to reach her in that place of profound sadness and grief. My aunt was extremely vocal in her denial of the repercussions of adoption-related loss in my life; given the fact she abducted me and could have gotten in serious trouble for it. She had to rationalize her own guilt by convincing me and everyone around her that the adoption had no adverse effect on me whatsoever. Ironically her denial only compounded my trauma— along with being raised as "handicapped," since that was her personal scapegoat for my behavioral problems.

These inconsistent relationships can also be a manifestation of adoption trauma, divided loyalties (similar to those of children of divorced parents), and the resulting ambivalence. Adoptees may have a sense of not being "good enough" for a friend or a significant other; after all, they weren't good enough for their natural mother to keep, or good enough to deserve the truth that the adoptive parents kept from them.

Karen—The feeling of being not good enough for your mother to keep you, or being rejected and given away, is the painful core of the adoptee's wound. Many adoptees will never allow themselves to feel this, while others are overwhelmed and flooded by it.

Whether or not we are adopted, all of us must heal the injuries that our parents inflicted on us as a result of their own unhealed wounds and limitations. Lack of self-esteem and self-confidence, or a poor sense of self, are not limited to adoptees. However, adoptees bear the particularly agonizing burden of feeling rejected by the one person in the world who is supposed to love you unconditionally: your mother. Some of the deepest healing work that must be done is to fully realize and accept that how one's parents treated you is not a reflection of our own worth, but a reflection of them (their wounds and also the places they were whole.)

Jodi—I'm starting to come to that place now. With my aunt adopter, it was all about the way I reflected on her. She treated me more like an accessory than a separate human being. I remember her trying to hug me in public—for the sake of appearances, *look how close we are*—and I didn't let her; she'd take it as a personal insult. She wanted her own little MiniMe, but I was my father's child, not hers, and had enough of him in me to be the total opposite of her ideal daughter. The irony is that my aunt allowed me to grow up believing my mother didn't want me, that she rejected me and put me up for adoption, when in fact she did nothing of the sort. My mother didn't even know I'd been in my aunt's custody for a year until she got the request-to-adopt papers in the mail. Was my aunt so insecure that she couldn't risk my having even occasional written contact with my mother?

When I reestablished contact my dad, when I was twelve, I completely rejected my uncle adopter as any kind of parent. But I think I'd already done that from the beginning, since I had my dad in my life up until the adoption. My aunt admitted that she was afraid I'd reject her in the same way if she "allowed" me to meet my mother, so she held off on that until I reached my mid-twenties. I think adoption reunion doesn't cause a loss of loyalty; so much as it brings to the forefront what has always lurked in the background. You can't lose what you've never had. If the adoptive relationship isn't close after reunion with one or both natural parents, it's probably safe to say it wasn't very close beforehand either.

Overly controlling or self-centered adoptive parents may manipulate or terminate relationships in the "best interest" of the adoptee. Friendships can be severed if the friend is not "our kind of people." Dating relationships may be deemed inappropriate, perhaps out of fear the adopted daughter will repeat the mistakes of her unwed teenage mother. Counseling may come to an abrupt end if the therapist wants to explore post-adoption issues in more depth, or asks for more disclosure about the adoption. Adult friends or mentors may be rejected if the adoptive parent fears them becoming replacement mother or father figures. The adoptee may or may not be warned of this, and either way, the rejection can reinforce the sense of not being good enough—the reminder of being relinquished or abandoned.

It's important for the adoptee to reach an understanding of the adoptive parents' personal failures and shortcomings, rather than internalizing them. Narcissistic, controlling adoptive mothers may harbor a secret jealousy that a daughter will find and prefer her natural mother, thus withholding vital information or interfering in reunion. She may obstruct other relationships with attachment potential, such as mentors or counselors. I've mentioned my "spiritual mother," who became a close friend during my high school years. She invested a lot of her time in being a friend and mentor to young people, and has had more positive impact on my own life than anyone else. My aunt often said things that made me question her friendship and feel as if I was a burden to my spiritual mother, rather than someone she wanted to spend time with. The power of suggestion can be really strong for someone who doesn't have much self-esteem. Instead of trusting my spiritual mom and believing in her loyalty, I would accuse her of not caring about me, of staying in my life because of a sense of obligation or duty and not because she genuinely liked me. Ironically, I saw the same thing in my aunt, that she raised me out of obligation to my dad and their parents and a duty to keep me in the family, instead of because she wanted a child. There was always something missing between my aunt and myself, emotional connection, unconditional love, or maybe just the freedom to choose where my loyalties should lie.

While this fear of abandonment can create a sense of impending doom in relationships, based on the experience that people can suddenly and inexplicably turn their back on you, it's important to remember that the ones who sincerely care enough to stay in your life will do so to the extent of their capabilities. Adoptive mothers cannot exert their will over everyone or remain in control of their children's lives forever.

Karen—Overall, what Jodi is sharing with us here is her current narrative about herself and her life. She interweaves what part of her life story is about being adopted, what is about the impact of being raised by her adoptive parents/aunt/uncle, and what is about how she has become the person she is today and continues to become.

We become close to people by telling them our story. Where we come from. Who we are. How we got to be this way. It is by sharing the story of our self, and listening to the story of the other, that we create the story of "us." To fully tell their story, adoptees need to know the truth of who they are and their value as human beings. And as we all know, the truth will set you free. It also is the bedrock of intimacy.

* * *

Karen Caffrey, LPC, JD is a Licensed Professional Counselor, a certified Somatic Experiencing Practitioner, a writer, a reunited adoptee, and an attorney. She has a private psychotherapy practice in West Hartford, Connecticut, and invites you to visit her at *www.karencaffrey.com* and on Facebook, "Karen Caffrey Counseling." One of her specialties is counseling adult adoptees. Karen is also President of Access Connecticut Now, Inc., a grassroots organization that successfully lobbied for a 2014 law that has restored the right of post-1983 adoptees to access their original birth certificates. Karen and Access Connecticut remain committed to restoring the right of all Connecticut adoptees to know the truth about their origins.

Jodi Haywood is an adoptee in reunion, a wife, mom, stepmom, writer, and marathon runner. Taken from her native Britain at age two, she grew up in a closed relative adoption which, while psychologically damaging, greatly influenced her storytelling abilities. Her writing credits include two "slightly twisted" young adult novels (and many more in the works), a church history book, contributions to adoption anthologies, and her memoir/case study work-in-progress, *Attachment Unavailable*, which has its own Facebook page. She recently returned to college to complete a psychology degree, with the goal toward a career in post-adoption/developmental trauma therapy.

CHAPTER 11—BEAUTY, CONTROL, AND ADOPTION

By Mila C. Konomos

ACCRETION

I.

the fat drips.
the stalagmite:
horror of accretion.
conical elevation
inserts a dominance.
lovely.
my two mamas will meet.
in the Fallopian corridor.
one mother, the conception.
one mother, the virgin.
(God and my mother—
stole my tongue. God and my mother—
replaced it with a new one)
first lap of the white lard.
shift in my sleeves and
thumb.

the marrow will return.

II.

with its incision. and
emaciation.
cells—immaculate.
indivisible.
until the stalactite ceases.
and the fat
completes the migration.
viscera to dissolution.
wave, mothers.
dominance of the marrow—

my favorite friend

———

Below is the postulated equation for optimal attainment of the White American Standard of Unequivocal Beauty (UB)*:
UB = [Celery + Carrots = CC] x [Obsessive Exercising = OE] x [Large Boobs (LB) + Round Eyes (RE) + Blonde Hair (BH) + Long Legs (LL)] – [All Things Asian (ATA)]

   *All the above factors of the equation must be applied. Although various measurements of each factor may be applied, no substitutions are permitted. Substitutions or omissions will render the UB factor void. Decreasing the CC and OE factors while increasing LB, RE, BH, and LL factors will produce optimal results. If one can manipulate the ATA factor to equal zero, the UB factor will reach its most desirable state. *Warning*: When lacking vital components for the above equation, proceed with caution. An imbalanced equation may produce sub-optimal results potentially producing harmful byproducts including SB [SB = Skin and Bones] and even D [D = Death].

* * *

I used to believe that I could force myself to become something I am not.

I used to believe that the above equation, if applied flawlessly, was the answer to my suffering, my sorrow, my perceived inferiority. The equation was my solution to the problem of being me. Of being Yellow in a White World. Of being Lost in a Found World. Of being Taken even though I never asked to be Given. Of forfeiting every piece of myself because that was what others decided was best for me. Of losing complete control over my fate at the hands of those who thought they had a better grasp of my destiny.

I wanted to believe that I had the power to be whoever I wanted to be—because I was raised to believe that it doesn't matter who you were born to be or to whom you were born. Ultimately, I was trained to think that all that mattered was who others taught me I was supposed to be.

* * *

Hence, I worked compulsively to perfect what components of the equation I could control.

It became my religion.

By the age of sixteen, I had perfected my eating and exercising habits to a scientific precision of routine and counting. Ten carrot sticks in the morning. Ten celery sticks at lunch time. One hour of running, followed by one hour of swimming, followed by starving and starving and more starving.

I was genius in the manipulation and application of the first half of the equation. But it was the second half of the equation that presented far greater difficulty. It seemed that nature would bend, but only so far. Nonetheless, I got it to bend as far as I possibly could.

I got it to bend down to ninety pounds. I got it bend all the way to amenorrhea. To hair loss and adult lanugo. To freezing when it was eighty degrees outside.

But I could not bend the Asian out of me. I could not bend my legs to grow any longer. I could not bend my eyes to become any rounder. My hair stayed black as asphalt and my breasts as small as lemons.

And so my UB factor hovered, ever immobile, ever stagnant.

Yet I had doubtless conviction that the more intimately I approached skin and bones—even death—the closer I got to reaching Unequivocal Beauty.

I even willingly came under the knife.

Is not the ultimate sacrifice to the idol of beautiful to brush lips with death that one may approach immortal exquisiteness?

* * *

I am not seeking pity or even sympathy.

I am simply illustrating the truth that to what we are exposed is what we believe we must be—until we are hopefully fortunate enough to finally realize otherwise.

* * *

Although I recognize now that I cannot bend myself to become something I am not, I am still attempting to realize the otherwise—

I think perhaps it is because I have yet to also fully comprehend that I do not have to choose between one self and the other, and that ultimately, I will never belong to one or the other.

I am of two worlds.

* * *

Yet when you belong neither here nor there, in some ways, the answers you seek will always elude you.

But my hope is that in other ways, we can eventually stumble our way to them.

* * *

Ultimately, what was I was trying to bend myself to become? Obviously, I knew that I could not make myself White. Yet I came to lament so intensely that I had not been born the ideal White woman, that I believe my anorexia was a manifestation of an intense self-hate of not only my body, but of my entire appearance, and ultimately, my irrevocable Asianness.

How was I supposed to grow up in a White family within a White World and *not* wish I was White? Did I ever have a chance of growing up not wishing that my body wasn't my body, wishing that my face was not my face?

Even if my parents had been racially sensitive or had possessed an inkling of a clue about how growing up the only non-White person in a predominantly White World would affect a person's self-image, the fact that I was surrounded by White people, White media, White everything at all times made certain that I would grow up hating the color of my skin, the shape and color of my eyes, the blackness of my hair.

Even if my parents had told me every day of my life that I was beautiful and that being Asian was beautiful (my mom and dad did often tell me I was pretty), White parents telling their Asian daughter that she is pretty begins to feel like a lie when her experiences teach her that being an Asian girl is a curse of ugliness, exotification, and exclusion.

I never saw myself reflected in the most important figures in my life. I never saw myself reflected in books or movies. When I did, they were negative stereotypes that made me feel ashamed of everything that made me Asian.

But most importantly, I never saw myself reflected in my own mother—a blonde, blue-eyed, tall, statuesque, Nordic-looking woman. When she told me I was beautiful—with my short and petite stature, flat-chest, flat-face, slanted almond eyes, bridgeless nose, hair black like an oil spill, skin like burnt butter—I could not look at her and see myself reflected in her beauty. We looked nothing alike.

It is hard to express just how profoundly it affected me when I gazed into the mirror and saw what stared back at me—and that the image that I saw did not match the images of the people I called family, friends, neighbors, schoolmates.

Even to this day, no matter how many times I hear, "Oh, but you are so beautiful," it is immediately deflected as insincere flattery born of pity and condescension. Not that I do not want to believe it. But rather I have been indoctrinated not to believe it. Not intentionally but inevitably.

You cannot grow up in a society that values Whiteness over all other colors and races and ethnicities and hope to develop a healthy self-image without the support of a family and community of your own that teaches you to inherently value what you look like. But transracial adoptees often lack just that. If you never see yourself reflected in positive ways in your family and community, you are destined to grow up with some degree of insecurity and self-loathing regarding your appearance.

And that's exactly what happened with me as a transracial, transnational adoptee growing up in both a family and community that was White American. It should not be surprising or anomalous that such an upbringing had profound effects on my identity and self-image, and ultimately my psychological health.

But being the only Asian person among a predominantly White community and family is not the only factor that contributed to my development of anorexia.

As the years have passed and I have emerged from the "adoption fog," I have come to realize that although my anorexia was in part about appearance and trying to bend myself into someone I was not, it was ultimately never about food or weight.

It was about my adoption. It was about control—or the lack thereof.

It was about my loss and grief and the circumstances over which I had no control that determined I would grow up severed and lost from my original family, country, people, culture, and language.

My anorexia was my medicine. My self-inflicted starvation was my coping mechanism—my wholehearted attempt to feel in control. My attempt to discipline my pain, force my grief to submit, numb my loss. It was the muzzle to silence, the reins to control all the emotions that were not allowed to come out, but felt as though they were constantly howling and bucking at the gate.

I could not control the fact that I had no knowledge of who I was or from whom I had come. I could not control the truth that I never knew who my Korean mother was or why she had abandoned me. I could not control all of the racism and prejudice that I experienced amongst "my" predominantly White community. I could not control all the relocating and the repeated loss of friendships and familiarity. I had no control over my life's circumstances.

So, I found something I could control. Growing up in a home where appearance was of the utmost importance—diets were the norm and perfectionism was the way—anorexia almost came naturally, easily, logically to me.

I learned that appearance was power. And power was control.

So in my subconscious mind if I could make myself appear a certain way, then I would be superior. I would have the power for which I longed. I could gain the sense of control that had eluded me since the day I was born.

The more weight I lost, the more in control, the more empowered I felt. It was addicting. The thrill, the rush I felt when I stepped on the scale and saw that I had lost another pound. The smaller the number, the greater my sense of power.

My anorexia was my power.

It was exhilarating to feel as though I had this power, this control that no one else around me possessed and most importantly, that no one could take away from me. Of course, I realize now it was almost delusional, and absolutely any sense of power or control was nothing but illusion. But it was all that I felt that I had. It was the only way I could feel what I was so desperate to feel: in control of my life and myself.

The truth was that I was only becoming weaker and less in control. Any strength or power that I had was seeping away. The more I tried to become someone I was not, the more I tried to wield power over the truth and get it to submit to illusion, the more unhealthy and lost I became. The more I denied the profound, traumatic effects adoption had on my life, the more trapped and miserable I became.

Of course, at the time, I had no clue that my anorexia was a coping mechanism for dealing with the dormant and latent psychological, social, and familial issues resulting from being adopted. My family was even more clueless. None of us had any awareness of the complexities of adoption, and in particular the complications that come with transracial adoption. I just thought I was crazy.

Now, it makes so much sense.

On top of being an adoptee who had been relinquished as an infant without any say in my fate, I was adopted into a military family. We moved every one to two years. These were not the most ideal circumstances for an adoptee with attachment issues and a fear of abandonment and rejection. The constant moving added loss upon loss. Any notion of control over my own life became nonexistent.

My dad was gone at sea for indefinite periods of time. I never knew when he was coming back—or if he was coming back. Though it was simply his duty, this was very destabilizing and psychologically stressful for a deeply emotional, adopted child like myself.

Combine this instability with a tendency toward perfectionism, a strong focus on appearance within my family, and clear racial disparities—it was the perfect formula for developing anorexia as a coping mechanism.

* * *

Eventually, I overcame my anorexia in physiological terms but not psychologically. Although I was no longer clinically underweight, and the amenorrhea, lanugo, and other symptoms had subsided, controlling my weight remained a coping mechanism.

I ultimately became addicted to laxatives—a seemingly peculiar addiction. But again, it was all about grappling for a sense of order, a way to feel as though I was in control of something tangible. Laxatives helped me to maintain that illusion.

The addiction to laxatives ultimately arose from an almost universal trigger for adoptees—a traumatic break-up. After I graduated from college, I eventually got engaged to a guy I had been dating for almost two years. I had my dress. The church and photographers were reserved. The wedding party was lined up. Then, four months before the wedding, my fiancé broke up with me—without explanation. He simply told me he didn't think we should get married, didn't think we should date, and then he got up from the table and that was that. We never talked about it again. Six months later he was married, and I was left trying to make sense of it all.

The use of laxatives quite honestly began innocently. Due to the stress of the break-up, my body just seemed to shut down. So, I started using laxatives. But with a history like mine, I should have known I was entering dangerous territory. One can imagine how an event like a broken engagement could trigger deep-seated adoption issues of abandonment and rejection similar to that of an adoptee's original relinquishment, and hence, how desperation for control might manifest in unhealthy ways.

As I began to lose weight due to the stress, the memories of the sense of power and control that I had experienced when I was anorexic began to return and flood me emotionally. Slowly but surely I became dependent on laxatives as a way to control my weight and to feel empowered once more.

This lasted for years.

It was not until I eventually married and my husband and I decided to try to have children that I finally became motivated enough to overcome my dependence on laxatives. There were practical steps I had to take to heal my digestive system and body in order to be able to have children. And of course, I had to learn healthy ways to process my adoption issues to be able to implement the practical steps. It was a very difficult process, and one that is ongoing.

I still struggle from time to time with wanting to gain a [illusionary] sense of control by way of controlling what I eat and how much I weigh. And there have certainly been periods in my life when I have hovered at the borderline between anorexia and healthfulness. But I can honestly say that I have no desire to return to anorexia, and I would qualify my relationship with food and weight as generally healthy. To me, this is a satisfying victory with which I am quite content.

* * *

So, in the end, how did I overcome my anorexia and my addiction to laxatives?

The primary realization that has helped me to overcome my anorexia and to cope with my adoption over the years is learning to accept that I will never be in control—that control is ultimately an illusion. Even of those things that I think I can steer or command, I cannot, because life is just too wild, unpredictable and adventurous to submit to control.

But as it pertains to my adoption, I have most importantly had to learn to accept that there is nothing I can ever do to make it right. There is no amount of work or control that I can attempt that will ever bring me complete resolution or closure. This is the only way that I have found peace—to accept that I will never find complete peace over my relinquishment and adoption.

Many others have challenged me on this by telling me that I am wrong, or that I am somehow missing something or that something is wrong with me that I have accepted that I will never completely heal.

But again, my healing is not about control—and that, obviously, includes even letting go of a sense of control over my own process of healing. I cannot force myself to heal in the same way as others. I cannot force myself to feel peace. Rather, for me, it has been about letting go of control and realizing for me personally that complete healing is not my goal, but rather acceptance of all the loose ends and open wounds and unresolved losses and griefs that will always be a part of my life and who I am.

This is my way to healing.

This is my way to being free of anorexia.

This is my way of realizing that control is something I will never have—whether adopted or not adopted, whether Asian or White—I have to let go.

Not of the sorrow and pain and grief, but rather of the expectation, the pressure, the demand that I should either never feel such deep emotion, or only feel them once in my life and then move on.

Being an adoptee is a journey for sure, but not one that is linear or simple.

It is complex and convoluted.

And I'm tired of trying to control it.

All I can do is allow myself to feel what is true.

To me, that is peace, that is healing, that is the only "control" that matters—not trying to control my circumstances to avoid the pain, but freeing myself from the control of others so that I can run toward it, heart-first, and embrace every bittersweet moment, every engulfing emotion that I am fortunate enough to experience now that I am no longer so paralyzed and entrapped by having to control it all.

Because ultimately that's what the anorexia was about for me—trying to avoid feeling all the pain, sorrow, joy, hurt, hope, love, grief that came with being adopted.

I had to accept that there is no equation—not only for attaining an illusion of ideal beauty, but even more significantly, no equation for managing and controlling the depth of emotion and pain that I have experienced as a transracial adoptee.

My equation for beauty and power was nothing but a hindrance, a poison that kept me emotionally stunted and miserable. It was born out of fear—a fear of feeling, because I was so afraid that if I allowed myself to feel, I would be crushed beneath the burden. I was afraid I would weep so uncontrollably that I would never be able to stop, that the grief would feel so dark that I would never see the light again.

Yet, I have discovered the truth to be quite the opposite. The more I allow myself to feel all of it, the closer I move toward psychological health. And although I still have my moments of weakness, of rage, of fear, more and more these moments give way to strength, vulnerability, tears, which ultimately, can only come when I choose to accept that control is an illusion that too often stands in the way of experiencing true love and whole health.

The more I let go of control, the more I open my heart and mind to feel all the darkness and pain that I feared for so long, the more courage and hope and love and resilience I find—in the end, the more light has opportunity to fill my life.

* * *

Mila C. Konomos is a reunited Korean American transracial adult adoptee. She was born in Seoul, Korea in 1975 and adopted six months later by a White American family. She has been in reunion with her Korean family since 2009. She and her husband have two children. Mila blogs at *The Lost Daughters* and *Yoon's Blur*

Chapter 12—Co-Dependency in Adoptees

By Lisa Floyd and Corie Skolnick, M.S. LMFT

My name is Lisa Floyd, and I am an adoptee who has recently reunited with both sides of my birth families. Writer and therapist, Corie Skolnick, and I are going to be discussing co-dependency as it relates to adoptees and how attachment is linked to co-dependency. Co-dependency is a term that is highly used in our culture, but for the purposes of this discussion it refers to the tendency that adoptees have to over attach to others due to a lack of bonding with the birth mother.

The origins of the concept of co-dependency

Lisa—Intimacy is hard for many people, but it is particularly hard for adoptees who might have issues of mistrust and abandonment. We hear the term, "co-dependent" used so much these days that it has pretty much become a cliché, but one can argue that adoptees are more susceptible to becoming co-dependent due to the trauma that they suffer at the beginning of their lives. I have friends who are adopted who think they are co-dependent and others who say they are not. I have done a great deal of research and reading about co-dependency, and I do not see how an adoptee can escape being co-dependent. As an adoptee myself, I certainly believe I fall

189

into this category. I look at the way adoptees relate to others, and I see behaviors that can be called co-dependency. We lose our other half at the beginning of our lives and in essence our ability to form secure attachments, so I am wondering if co-dependency does not become an issue because we have no sense of identity and therefore look to latch onto another to try to fill that need. It is very interesting to be able to talk to you and get your take on this as a mental health professional.

Corie—You are on to something here, Lisa! I have been around the mental health trenches long enough to remember a time when there was no such thing as the concept of "co-dependency" in terms of a discrete mental disorder that required treatment. Co-dependence is a relatively new malady. It did not even exist back in the day. The term itself evolved directly from the burgeoning twelve step movements of the 1970s. You probably already know that the twelve steps originated in the 1930s with Alcoholics Anonymous. All of the subsequent twelve step programs have their origins in AA, such as Co-Dependents Anonymous. Initially, the focus of all of them was an individual's addiction to some substance or some activity and the individual's "powerlessness" over that particular thing. It was not until 1979 that a discrete twelve step program formed to address the relational aspects of addiction. The first of these was called Adult Children of Alcoholics and obviously it was a group that addressed the issues common to that population. It included a group of people who felt addicted to *other people*. The first step of ACA was altered: "We admitted we were powerless over *others*." (Not alcohol.)

It did not take too long for people to understand that not every family that manifested the negative patterns found in addictive family systems had members with addiction problems. It was generally recognized that the problem of co-dependency existed *within the family member who did not have a substance disorder*. The phenomenon identified as co-dependency also existed in systems *without addictions present*. These important recognitions represented a major paradigmatic shift. With an identification of the features of co-dependency exclusive of addiction, the "co" became the identified mental health patient. So, the "co" became the focus of treatment. This shift in theory recognized that **trauma was the causative factor** and while it is reasonable to suppose that living in a family system where addiction is present will be to a greater or lesser degree traumatic, it is certainly true that not all trauma involves chemical addiction. I agree with you that the separation of an infant from its mother and maybe father, too, is a traumatic event.

So, the term and the disorder, co-dependency, both have early roots in addiction theory. But, that is only the beginning part of the story.

Historically, the features of what we now call co-dependence were not seen as problematic by everyone. Back in the day, before feminism galvanized American women around the notion that they were equal to men and should be treated by society as equal, the primary features of co-dependency were the hallmarks of "the good little wife." Patterns of people-pleasing, perfectionism, and selflessness were seen as virtues in women and especially in wives, and in some quarters they still are.

Also, for the most part, prior to the 1960s, the notion of individuation and differentiation as qualities of a healthy family system was very foreign.

So, the rise of feminism, the development of family systems theory—with an emphasis on the individual, and the recognition that early childhood trauma leads to personality and interpersonal dysfunction, all formed the bedrock of how we understand co-dependence.

This understanding of codependence has continued to evolve within the organization that now calls itself CoDA (Co-Dependents Anonymous). Instead of defining co-dependence in absolute terms, CoDA has instead assembled what they call, "The Patterns and Characteristics of Codependence." These patterns include denial, low self-esteem, compliance, control, and avoidance. Typically, this is what these patterns sound like when a co-dependent individual expresses them: He has difficulty identifying what he is feeling. He judges what he thinks, says or does harshly, as never good enough. He puts aside his own interests in order to do what others want. He freely offers advice and direction to others without being asked. He uses indirect or evasive communication to avoid conflict or confrontation.

Lisa—That sounds exactly like almost every adoptee I know, including myself! We as adoptees come into this world longing to be loved and nurtured by the mothers whom we developed inside for nine months, and then they are just gone. We are not allowed the opportunity to bond and attach to our other half, and I believe this causes an inordinate amount of damage which many of us continue to struggle with in our adult lives. We have no choice in the matter and are left wondering what is wrong with us because we are so deathly afraid of intimacy and cannot seem to form healthy attachments to others. I know in my case the lack of control that I had over that very crucial aspect of my life has lead me to try to control everyone and everything that I possibly can which leads to a great deal of heartache and dysfunctional relationships. How can the adoptee not be the classic co-dependent? Can you touch more on how you believe that the separation from the birth mother is a trauma of the highest order?

The relationship between co-dependency, trauma, and adoption

Corie—Well, I know many people will say, "Trauma of the highest order? What? What are you talking about, Lisa? What about missing limbs, birth defects, war, or pestilence? Those things are traumatic, but not adoption! Babies do not even **know** they have been relinquished if someone does not tell them that they were."

Have you heard this from people who do not want to acknowledge infant/maternal separation as traumatic? I certainly have. I have heard it from adoptees themselves who deny the impact of trauma in their own lives.

Certainly we all have a slightly different definition of the word, trauma. Let us use the one I typically employ when teaching: *"An emotional wound or shock that creates substantial lasting damage to the psychological development of a person."* (The American Heritage College Dictionary).

Is it fair to say that separating an infant from his/her mother is a shock or a wound? The two strongest inborn drives are known to be the drive to attach and the drive to avoid pain. These drives surpass even hunger, and we have known this about humans and all primates since the Harlow primate studies empirically proved as much at the University of Wisconsin at Madison dating back to the 1950s (Harlow, et al., 1971). Maternal deprivation in those earliest studies resulted in severe independent, behavioral, and psychological impairments in both the infants and the mothers and also notable permanent damage in interpersonal behaviors within the primate society. The paradox that you describe—extreme yearnings for attachment but chronic fears of closeness—sounds like you are stuck in the drama of negotiating those two powerful drives. It is almost as if you cannot escape the original experience of the frustrated attachment and intense pain of abandonment from that primary relationship.

Furthermore, recent advances in the field of neuroscience have allowed us to track and image actual developmental changes in the brains of human babies and in particular the brains of babies that have been deprived of maternal (biological mother) care. One of the latest findings is significant damage to the area of the brain known as the *corpus callosum*, a wide, flat bundle of neural fibers beneath the cortex. It connects the left and right cerebral hemispheres and facilitates inter-hemispheric communication. Abnormality in this structure has been linked to the Autism spectrum disorders which are, as we now know, primarily communication disorders. It is now widely believed that mild damage to the *corpus callosum* is responsible at an organic level for a lot of interpersonal pathology (Boger-Megiddo, et al., 2006). If relinquished infants are prone to this kind of organic damage developmentally, then the trauma that we talk about occurring after separation is not only psychological but it is very possibly physiological, too. One conclusion is that the collection of symptoms that relate to the trauma of adoption is actually describing the real trauma of organic brain damage.

Healing from adoption trauma

Lisa—Wow! I have never heard the trauma of adoption referred to as organic brain damage before, and I find that fascinating. Our brains are changed by trauma in ways science is only beginning to understand, but how do we get clinicians to realize it is not all in our heads? There must be more education about the effects of separation trauma on the infant so adoptees can receive the help they so desperately need and not suffer needlessly in silence. I am going to become an adoption therapist because I am tired of people not understanding, and I feel like my experience and empathy will help me

relate to those I want to help and to establish this as a
serious issue to study. How do we recover from organic
brain damage and not feel compelled to suffer through
behaviors we have just learned to cope with? I would say
a lot of adoptees are stuck in the paradox you refer to,
but how do we get unstuck? Therapy is crucial, but it
does not undo all the damage done by the trauma. How
can we learn to be healthy, functioning adults who thrive
in our lives without always feeling like the ugly duckling
who was not wanted?

Corie—Medical science has a very long way to go
before we can pinpoint *exactly* where physiology has gone
awry under conditions that we refer to as traumatic. Just
because we have this new and exciting research that does
seem to demonstrate real organic structural anomalies
developing under trauma conditions, the research is not
at all 100% conclusive. (Nothing is ever 100%.) As with
all brain research, a lot of what we think we are looking at
is still conjecture and far from universal. It is also just a
small piece of the puzzle that is co-dependency in
adoptees.

Anyway, the whole point of such research should
be prevention and treatment. In medicine I do not think
you will find too many medical practitioners who would
even consider wading into the waters of prevention in the
realm of adoption. In certain factions within the adoption
community itself, prevention of infant trauma looks like
family preservation, a fancy term that means: keep the
infants with their biological mothers and for some, this
means at all costs. So, prevention gets into politics and
economics and even religious realms that, so far, very few
are willing to tread. Even social workers can seem
reluctant to weigh in when it comes to the politics of
adoption. These recent findings about the preventable
tragedy that is infant brain trauma caused by maternal
infant separation will not come to bear in any realistic
way until the politics of adoption improves.

In medicine, currently, the predominant view of treatment most often means matching an appropriate medication to whatever symptoms a patient complains about. Even in psychology, a diagnosis that can be demonstrated to be organic, will most of the time result in a prescription for medicine, or at least an evaluation by a medical practitioner to rule out a need for a drug. Imagine a drug prescription for co-dependency!

Although that seems farfetched, the cluster of symptoms that relate to co-dependency, (through a medical lens) can easily be seen, especially when chronic, as depression or anxiety, and therefore warranting of medication. In fact, many adoptees self-refer to their doctors for anti-depressants and anxiolytics. Also, how many adoptees do you know who self-medicate with alcohol or other substances, not to mention self-injurious activities like over-eating, gambling, spending, or promiscuous sexual behaviors, etc.?

I have heard a lot of adoptees express that these attempts (whether they are medicine that is prescribed by a physician or a self-attempted strategy simply to somehow get some relief from the negative feelings), do not ever seem to work long term because they never address the root issue of abandonment. It is the number one critical complaint I hear about therapists. Typically, the therapist fails to acknowledge the adoptee's early trauma, or else he or she minimizes or dismisses entirely the lingering effects of separation.

So, in terms of treatment, not so much prevention, how do we incorporate these new findings from neuro-scientific research?

I think you are onto something important when you mention your desire to provide other adoptees with real empathy. Did you know that research has been conducted on the efficacy of many therapeutic orientations and the single most important factor in patient improvement is known to be a truly empathic experience? (Segilman, 1995) In other words, a therapist's philosophical orientation is less important than the genuine empathy they are able to provide in the treatment. What heals is the relationship, and it is never too late for the healing to begin.

Insight and knowledge about trauma are great, maybe even necessary, for a therapist to have to adequately undertake the treatment of a co-dependent adoptee, but I and many others believe that genuine repair to the brain of the once-traumatized infant, now stuck adult, only comes inside of the actual experience of really being *known* and *held in true regard* by "the other." Some say that this repair is conducted in the domain of the right brain of both patient and clinician. It is as if the right hemispheres of each brain are communicating something beyond language that was denied the infant when he/she was separated from the mother (Ross, 2000; Schore, 2003).

It is really important, even critical, to remember that not all adoptees develop co-dependent traits and certainly all people who identify as co-dependent were not exposed to infant trauma or adopted. So, let us not reduce co-dependency to anything so simple. The cluster of behaviors that are known as "co-dependency" have much, maybe more, to do with the interpersonal environment that the individual developed within. The conditions of these co-dependence-producing environments are well known. One commonality among these family systems is what we call the "parentification" of the child. The term "adult child" refers to a child raised by adults who reversed the roles in the family making the child (or children) precociously mature. Often these children were charged with responsibilities for themselves and younger siblings that allowed the parent to be neglectful. The "adult child" is recognized by a pseudo maturity. They have been given more responsibility than they should have ever had and therefore they never successfully acquired the skills and tools they needed for normal development. These faulty parenting conditions are required and necessary to be productive of a "parentified" child. However, parentification can be conducted on a continuum from "once in a great while" to "almost constantly." Parentification can mean very real neglect as in a failure to provide the concrete necessities of life or the more abstract and psychically destructive failure to provide security, or appropriate discipline, or even love. One classic example would be an adoptive parent who constantly implores reassurance from the child that he/she is the "real" parent. All children, even those within intact biological family systems will develop abnormally under those family conditions.

Perhaps, a traumatized infant is predisposed to be more vulnerable to relatively permanent effects of a family system that is productive of co-dependency. Perhaps, because of early trauma, such a person is predisposed to developing co-dependent traits as a result of damage to the parts of the brain that might otherwise be more flexible and resistant to interpersonal pathology. Where another kid could shrug off the effects of what we call "parentification," it is possible that the trauma victim has no such resiliency.

In terms of both causes of and treatment for co-dependency, I think it is crucial to understand the complexity of the syndrome and the possible relationship between it and adoption. It is tempting to reduce things down and to simplify, but that is hazardous. It is a big, complicated picture and every single experience is completely unique, so while we do look for commonality in service of our understanding, we have to strive to let every unique individual have his or her own experience. This is especially true for people who identify as co-dependents. The root of co-dependence is the deprivation of a self. In part, that is why treatment of co-dependency is so tricky. You have to challenge patients' assumptions and sometimes even their reality without denying their experience. That is sometimes hard to do. The paradox that is co-dependency is a real puzzle.

Many therapists I know say that treating co-dependency is the hardest thing. It definitely presents a

bind. When I was a very novice therapist I went to a
conference on co-dependency put on by the Hazelden
Foundation. The presenter was a renowned physician in
the field of chemical dependency treatment. I will never
forget his assertion that co-dependency was "a thousand
times more difficult to treat" than chemical dependency.
This opinion was echoed many years later by a colleague,
also a renowned therapist, when he said to a group of
therapists, "I would rather have a hundred addicts on my
caseload than one co."

     Lisa—I understand that therapy is the key to
getting to the root of our subconscious memories that
keep us stuck in behaviors of the past. We must go into
the deep and repressed memories that are terrifying to the
infant-self to truly find our freedom. It is fascinating to
think that brain repair can happen between the patient
and therapist. What kind of a therapist should we look
for, and what are signs that the person we are working
with is doing more harm than good? They need to have
done their own work in order not to project their needs
onto us. When is a good time to say goodbye to a
therapist?

     I think it is very unfair to label any one group as
being co-dependent, but it is compelling to look at the
similar behaviors displayed by adoptees and try to
understand what the commonality is. I believe I have
exhibited co-dependent traits because I did not know
who I really was. I had to reunite with my birth family
and find out about the beginning of my life in order to
feel connected to myself and the world. I have my
missing pieces, and I feel like I can move forward into a
future that I am very excited about.

     Corie—You raise some thorny issues here. First,
I will try to answer your question about the "kind" of
therapy that is most effective. If we are assuming that
your history includes infant trauma due to maternal loss
in infancy (or later), and/or your complaints obviously

relate to PTSD (Post-Traumatic Stress Disorder), I would recommend checking in to some of the short term therapeutic modalities that have developed relatively recently to treat trauma. Although I will not be able to adequately describe the evolution of even just one in the space we have here, I think it is fair to say that all of these have in common the goal of resolving past trauma at the level of the body/mind connection.

The oldest and most rigorously researched of these is probably EMDR (Eye Movement Desensitization and Reprocessing). EMDR (developed by Francine Shapiro in the late 1980s) has been around for over twenty years now and that is long enough to have an impressive body of research into its efficacy. Currently, EMDR therapy is internationally recognized as an effective form of trauma treatment. It is quite easy these days to find a therapist who has at least some training in EMDR.

Another reportedly potent therapy comes from the life's work of Peter Levine and also focuses on short term relief from symptoms that relate to trauma (both acute and chronic). Levine's treatment is known as Somatic Experiencing (trademark name SE).

Roger Callahan was another clinician who developed and trademarked a therapeutic intervention aimed at "stress" resolution. TFT, or Thought Field Therapy, is similar in some ways to the others, but different in that it has been marketed as a kind of "do it yourself" intervention as well as offered to "lay" people and not restricted to professional mental health practitioners. You can buy a video demonstration to DIY. The TFT organization is headed by Dr. Callahan's wife at present, and their website describes the treatment as, "a meridian tapping therapy that uses nature's healing system to balance the body's energy system."

I personally know therapists who have trained in one or more of all three of these interventions, and they are all clinicians I trust and would refer a patient to with an unqualified recommendation. But, remember that any therapist should also have a good grasp of family systems theory, too. That would be an ideal package.

That brings us to the second part of your question. What kind of therapist should you look for and what are the signs they are doing more harm than good? Then, when should you say goodbye?

Again, this is a tricky question. If you have serious or even persistent mental health issues (and these can manifest in your life as interpersonal issues), I say, yes, get professional help. And by professional, I mean someone who has advanced training and licensure in psychology and comes highly recommended by someone you know to be reliable. Do your homework. Do not be afraid to shop. You are buying a professional service and you want the best. You might be limited by insurance concerns and other factors, but I do think it is important to look for a therapist with impeccable credentials. That does not guarantee that you will "click" though, so be prepared to ask some questions and know what the answers mean. You need to realize that not every therapist is right for every client. You may need to interview a few before you find a good fit.

The tricky part comes into play when you start working together. There is an old Gestalt saying that goes, "No pain, no gain." This refers to the fact that an honest examination of your past and especially your present will most likely be somewhat uncomfortable, but a good therapist will challenge your assumptions in the service of your growth. That is going to make you mad. You DO want a therapist that holds you accountable and also encourages you to take responsibility for your life, even though that kind of change usually means some pain. This is why it is tricky. It is sometimes difficult to know whether you do not feel great after a session because the therapist called you on your dysfunction, or they are doing something wrong.

How do you know when a therapist's own issues are getting in the way of your therapy? Good question. Do not be afraid to ask him or her. The right answer is,

"I do not know. Let us look at that together. Maybe my issues are clogging up your therapy. Let us fix that. What makes you think so? How can we get back on track?" Just like any other profession, nobody is perfect and a therapist can make boo-boos. You just want one who does not get defensive and claim perfection if you feel something strange is going on. Defensiveness is a sure sign that it is time to say goodbye.

Lisa—I would add that I believe it is imperative that the therapist be someone who is familiar with adoption trauma and the complicated issues of grief and loss. I have so enjoyed our conversation and have learned a great deal from you. Thank you so much for talking with me.

Corie—I agree. I might even say that what is ideal is a therapist who has experience with working with adoptees, especially adoptees who identify with co-dependency specifically. You cannot overestimate the value of experience. On the other hand, sometimes a gifted novice who is willing to learn a lot and hustle to get up to speed by reading everything he or she can find and is willing to obtain advanced training can be very beneficial. Sometimes, if the chemistry is right between you and the right person, that is the ticket. In the end, I do believe that in treating the lingering symptoms of infant trauma, the primary curative factor is the felt sense of truly being known and being held in regard.

References

Boger-Megiddo I., DW Shaw, et. al. "Corpus Callosum Morphometrics in Young Children With Autism Spectrum Disorders," in *Journal of Autism and Developmental Disorders*, 36 (6): 733-739. DOI: 10-1007/s 10803-006-0121-2.

Callahan, Roger. *Callahan Techniques* blog, 2011, http://www.rogercallahan.com/.

"Co-Dependents Anonymous," CoDA, accessed September 3, 2014, http://coda.org/.

Harlow, H. F., M. K. Harlow, and S. J. Suomi. "From thought to therapy: Lessons from a primate laboratory," in American Scientist, 59 (5): 538-549. DOI: 1974-06718-001.

Ross, Colin A., *The Trauma Model: A Solution to the Problem of Comorbidity in Psychiatry*. Richardson, TX: Manitou Communications, Inc., 2000.

Schore, Allan N., *Affect Regulation and the Repair of the Self.* New York: W.W. Norton & Co., 2003.

Segilman, M. E. "The effectiveness of psychotherapy. The Consumer Reports study," in *American Psychologist*, 50 (12): 965-974. DOI: 8561380.

* * *

Lisa Floyd grew up in a closed adoption wondering who she was and where she came from. It took many years for her adoption fog to emerge after which she decided to search for and eventually reunite with both sides of her birth families. It is only in finding her birth families and what occurred in the beginning days of her life that she has found her identity and her voice. She is passionate about adoptee rights and plans on becoming an adoption therapist to help her fellow adoptees find their authentic selves and meaningful, purpose-filled lives. She is also a contributor to the upcoming anthology, *Adoptee Survival Guide*.

Corie Skolnick, M.S. LMFT was a marriage and family therapist in Los Angeles for more than twenty years, concurrently serving as an adjunct faculty member in the psychology departments of California State University, Northridge, and Moorpark College.

Her first novel, *Orfan* was selected by the prestigious Hugh C. Hyde Living Writers Series at San Diego State University (2012). *Orfan* was also a nominee for the 2012-2013 Freshman Common Reading Selection at California State University, Northridge.

Corie is a contributor to the anthology, *Adoption Reunion in the Social Media Age*, and a travel writer at the travel blog, *Desto3*.

America's Most Eligible, Corie's second novel, will be published in late 2014 by Mannequin Vanity Publishing/Mannequin Vanity Records (New York/San Diego).

AFTERWORD—
LIVING WITH OR WITHOUT
THERAPY: ITS EFFECT ON THE
WORLD

By Deanna Doss Shrodes

When I first learned that Laura Dennis was creating this anthology, I couldn't have been more ecstatic. *Adoption Therapy* is a groundbreaking book; one that I'm hoping will cause even one adoptee's experience to be different from my own.

The only healthy home I've experienced is the one I live in now with my husband and children. My natural family is fraught with issues and my adoptive home crumbled in dysfunction. Both of my mothers' life experiences rendered them emotionally scarred and in need of real help. My natural mother never got the kind of help she needed, and neither did my adoptive mother. The ramification of their choices—on me and upon others—cannot be underestimated or even fully qualified.

Strangely, both women would say they got the help they needed.

My now deceased natural mother maintained that she received counsel. But for all I can ascertain, it was from the maternity home/adoption agency where she relinquished me. She also referenced talking to a minister at one point. Neither of these options could hardly be considered adequate assistance for the trauma she endured. The "counseling" she received was commonplace for girls and women of the Baby Scoop Era. The extent of this "counseling" appeared to be an assurance that in relinquishing she would "move on" and "find a new start." For all of those promises, she never found emotional health and wholeness.

Growing up, I was keenly aware of the painful existence my adoptive mother lived and often pled for her to do something about it. What resulted was spiritual bypass. Bonnie Martin, MEd, CACS, LCPC says:

> *There is a little known psychological term called "spiritual bypass." Spiritual bypass is when we engage in religious beliefs and activities in order to avoid or cover up unmet needs, deep wounds or hidden fears.*

My adoptive mother's wounds were spiritually bypassed, as is common for Christians. My questions about her circumstance or requests for her to seek help were met with Christian clichés and standby scripture verses. As a teenager, I vividly remember saying to my adoptive mom, "Please mom, get some help. You need counseling!" to which she replied, "God is my strength!" I answered back with, "He really seems to be falling down on the job these days…" I'm surprised I didn't get immediately punished for such a retort, but I believe she was too emotionally spent at the time to dole out a consequence.

The extent of the help my adoptive mother pursued down through the years was from pastors of our local church. I am not against the church, in fact—I'm a part of it! I have served as a pastor for the last few decades, being educated and licensed and along with many or most other pastors, giving what would be referred to as spiritual guidance. However, we have our limitations. What we provide (unless one is a licensed professional counselor in addition to a pastor) is not the same as therapy. In the setting in which I was raised, it was not only acceptable but preferable to talk to a minister rather than a therapist. Growing up in a family that didn't seek therapy when it was sorely needed has now made me a huge fan of therapy! I determined early on that my children will have a different experience than mine.

There were several times throughout my adult life that I sought therapy. It wasn't always successful, as it took a while to find an adoption-competent therapist who recognized the significant loss, grief, and trauma that comes with adoption. The positive affect on my life once proper help was found cannot be fully expressed in words. Because of the competency and compassion of my therapist as well as the hard work I put in, my family has a quality of life we wouldn't have otherwise.

There will be those who bristle at the content of *Adoption Therapy*.

Some will resist the idea that post-adoption issues exist at all, or reject the idea of trauma as it relates to adoption, preferring to live in denial than seek appropriate help for themselves or their adopted son or daughter.

As a pastor, I can testify to the fact that the vast majority of congregants I have pastored over the years who struggle with infertility and come to me about it, have not been to therapy. And most have no intention to go. I have often pondered the fact that when many of these people choose to adopt, they do so without ever receiving appropriate help for their loss. Adoptees pay a steep price for this, so many times. I know I did.

I'm thankful that Laura Dennis has blown the lid off of secrecy and given the writers of *Adoption Therapy* a voice to share their experience. Because of her stewardship, what we have gone through is no longer swept under the carpet or forgotten. And she didn't just bring adoptees together to pour it all out unabated, but to join forces with therapists who could actually speak to our pain and do something about it.

It's my prayer that *Adoption Therapy* and books like it become required reading for any potential adoptive parent. Are some of our stories hard to read? You bet.

But unless one is willing to truly investigate the adoptee experience from an actual adoptee, I am highly suspect of his or her ability to parent an adoptee son or daughter effectively.

Sadly, my own two moms probably wouldn't have picked up a copy of *Adoption Therapy*, and made an attempt to learn, heal or change. I hope others will make the opposite choice. For themselves first, and then for all of the people they love, who love them too, and desperately want nothing more than whole, healed, family members.

This book underscores again and again that adoptees' feelings of loss and pain are not rare among those who share our experience. Hopefully in reading *Adoption Therapy*, adoptees who are ambivalent about therapy will realize what they can gain by pursuing it. It's the worth the investment of time and finances. The only regret I have about therapy is that I didn't find the right therapist sooner.

Living without therapy when you or your loved ones need it, is agonizing. Receiving the right kind of therapy can revolutionize everything in your personal world and in the world in general. When we receive what we need to be whole, we are all poised to be and do everything as intended by our Creator.

* * *

Deanna Doss Shrodes is a licensed minister with the Assemblies of God and has served as a pastor for twenty-six years, along with her pastor-husband, Larry. They have been married for twenty-six years, have three children and live in the Tampa Bay area where they co-pastor Celebration Church of Tampa. Deanna speaks at churches and conferences internationally and is also an accomplished musician, worship leader, songwriter, and certified coach. An award-winning writer, she is also a contributing author to *Chocolate For a Woman's Courage,*

(Simon & Schuster), a contributing author to *Lost Daughters: Writing Adoption from a Place of Empowerment and Peace* (CQT Media and Publishing), and the author of the book *Juggle: Manage Your Time, Change Your Life*.

Deanna blogs at *Adoptee Restoration* and contributes at *Lost Daughters* and *Adoption Voices Magazine*. She leads a search and support group, Adoptee Restoration Tampa Bay and is passionate about providing a safe place for adoptees to heal, as well as expanding the Christian community's understanding of adoption.

WHAT'S NEXT

Thank you so much for reading *Adoption Therapy, Perspectives from Clients and Clinicians on Processing and Healing Post-Adoption Issues.*

Want more?
Please go to
www.Laura-Dennis.com
There you can sign up to receive updates on
upcoming anthologies, and announcements for free
and discounted books.

If you are interested in participating in the forthcoming Part 2 of *Adoption Therapy*, email the Editor at laura@adoptedrealitymemoir.com with your essay topic.

Want to read more from adoptees, first moms and adoptive parents? Find *Adoption Reunion in the Social Media Age*, available in e-book and paperback on Amazon.

CONTRIBUTORS

Marcy Axness, Ph.D., author of *Parenting for Peace: Raising the Next Generation of Peacemakers*, is a leading authority in the fields of early human development, adoption, prenatal psychology, and interpersonal neurobiology. Using as a narrative foundation her experiences as an adoptee and a mother, she writes and speaks internationally on parenting, society, and the needs of children. One of the world's few experts in the primal issues involved in adoption, Dr. Axness has taught prenatal development at the graduate level and has a private practice coaching parents and "pre-parents" around the world. She is the mother of two peacemakers, Ian and Eve, both in their twenties. She invites you to join her at *MarcyAxness.com*.

Karen Belanger is an adult adoptee and the author of *Assembling Self,* an adoption poetry book, and writes at her blog of the same name. She contributes at The Lost Daughters and was recently included in the *Lost Daughters: Writing Adoption from a Place of Empowerment and Peace*. Karen has held various leadership positions within the adoption education, reform, and activism community over the past fifteen years. She is currently submitting pieces for two other adoption books and is working on her second book.

Karen Caffrey, LPC, JD is a Licensed Professional Counselor, a certified Somatic Experiencing Practitioner, a writer, a reunited adoptee, and an attorney. She has a private psychotherapy practice in West Hartford, Connecticut, and invites you to visit her at *www.karencaffrey.com* and on Facebook, "Karen Caffrey Counseling." One of her specialties is counseling adult adoptees. Karen is also President of Access Connecticut Now, Inc., a grassroots organization that successfully lobbied for a 2014 law that has restored the right of post-1983 adoptees to access their original birth certificates. Karen and Access Connecticut remain committed to restoring the right of all Connecticut adoptees to know the truth about their origins.

Lucy Chau Lai-Tuen, stage name Lucy Sheen –Made in Hong Kong, exported to the UK as a transracial adoptee in 1960s. A dyslexic actor, writer, filmmaker, who loves Dim sum, Yorkshire puddings and a nice cuppa cha! Lucy trained at the Rose Bruford College of Speech and drama and graduated in 1985. Her first professional job was the female lead in the ground breaking British-Chinese feature film, *Ping Pong* (1987). Her film credits include *Secrets & Lies, Something Good: The Mercury Factor*. Her published writing includes, *The Dance is New, Perpetual Child, An Adult Adoptee Anthology*, and *Adoptionland: From Orphan to Activist*. Lucy is currently developing several writing projects for stage and screen.

Laura Dennis (Editor) was born and adopted in New Jersey and raised in Maryland. She earned a B.A. and M.F.A. in dance performance and choreography, with a certificate in critical theory. She gave up aches and pains and bloody feet to become a sales director for a biotech startup. Then with two children under the age of three, in 2010 she and her husband sought to simplify their lifestyle and escaped to his hometown, Belgrade. While the children learned Serbian in their cozy preschool, Laura recovered from sleep deprivation and wrote *Adopted Reality, A Memoir*, available on Amazon.

An adoptee activist in reunion, she writes at The Lost Daughters, Adoption Voices Magazine and her own blog, *Expat (Adoptee) Mommy*. Her essays have been published in *Lost Daughters: Writing Adoption from a Place of*

Empowerment and Peace, The Perpetual Child, Dismantling the Stereotype, Adult Adoptee Anthology, and the soon-to-be-released *Dear Wonderful You, Letters to Adopted & Fostered Youth Around the World.* She is passionate about giving voice to the adoptee experience and is proud to have edited the popular anthology, *Adoption Reunion in the Social Media Age* (Entourage Publishing), along with several forthcoming titles.

Lisa Floyd grew up in a closed adoption wondering who she was and where she came from. It took many years for her adoption fog to emerge after which she decided to search for and eventually reunite with both sides of her birth families. It is only in finding her birth families and what occurred in the beginning days of her life that she has found her identity and her voice. She is passionate about adoptee rights and plans on becoming an adoption therapist to help her fellow adoptees find their authentic selves and meaningful, purpose-filled lives.

Rebecca Hawkes was adopted as an infant and is herself an adoptive parent by way of older-child foster adoption. She has presented on adoption-related topics at various venues. Her writing has appeared at the blogs, *Rebecca Hawkes, The Thriving Child, Lost Daugthers, Adoption Voices Magazine, BlogHer,* and *The Huffington Post,* and in the anthologies *Lost Daughters: Writing Adoption From a Place of Empowerment and Peace* and *Adoption Reunion in the Social Media Age.* She is certified as a parenting instructor by both the Beyond Consequences Institute and Gordon Training International. She is also a trained MotherWoman facilitator and a former assistant leader for The Center for Nonviolent Communication's Parent Peer Leadership Program.

Jodi Haywood is an adoptee in reunion, a wife, mom, stepmom, writer, and marathon runner. Taken from her native Britain at age two, she grew up in a closed relative adoption which, while psychologically damaging, greatly influenced her storytelling abilities. Her writing credits include two "slightly twisted" young adult novels (and many more in the works), a church history book, contributions to adoption anthologies, and her memoir/case study work-in-progress, *Attachment Unavailable*, which has its own Facebook page. She recently returned to college to complete a psychology degree, with the goal toward a career in post-adoption/developmental trauma therapy.

Lori Holden writes regularly at *LavenderLuz.com* about parenting and living mindfully and is a columnist at *The Huffington Post* and at the *Denver Post*'s moms site. She is the author of *The Open-Hearted Way to Open Adoption: Helping Your Child Grow Up Whole*, written with her daughter's birth mom and after listening to adult adoptees and first parents tell of their varied experiences. She lives in Denver with her husband and two tweens and speaks to adoption agencies and their clients about openness in adoption and giving equal access for all citizens to original birth records. She has been known to practice the Both/And mindset when it comes to red wine and dark chocolate.

Mila C. Konomos is a reunited Korean American transracial adult adoptee. She was born in Seoul, Korea in 1975 and adopted six months later by a White American family. She has been in reunion with her Korean family since 2009. She and her husband have two children. Mila blogs at *The Lost Daughters* and *Yoon's Blur*.

Kristi Lado was adopted through the closed domestic system in Pennsylvania. Formerly an associate producer for cable TV's *Forensic Files*, she has since become an independent writer and advocate for open records. Kristi has served as a board member for Adoption Forum of Philadelphia and volunteers for Pennsylvania Adoptee Rights (PAR). She recently co-founded C.A.R.E.S., an online support forum for those conceived by rape, and blogs about adoption issues at www.Aquarian Adoptee.com.

Lesli Maul, LCSW is a licensed clinical social worker whose career spans two and a half decades. The past 12 have been in private practice. She enjoys speaking to groups about courage, authenticity and wholehearted living. Each October she offers a workshop to adoptees entitled, "The Daring Way™ for Adult Adoptees: Our Strength is in Our Stories". Currently she is working on certification in Animal Assisted Psychotherapy.

She is a baby scoop era adoptee in reunion. She lives in Southern California with her husband and two sons. Other passions include her rescue animals (two dogs and one cat), gardening and quilting.

Brooke Randolph, LMHC, is a parent, therapist, and adoption professional with more than twenty years of experience working with children and families. She is a private practice counselor in Indianapolis, Indiana; the Vice President of PR, Outreach, and Communications at KidsFirst Adoption Services; and the mental health expert contributor at DietsInReview.com, a national diet and fitness column. She was a founding member of MLJ Adoptions, Inc., where she served as the VP of Social Services for seven years. She is a member of the Young Professionals Advisory Board for The Villages of Indiana, Inc., a child and family services agency that serves over 1,400 children and their families each day. She adopted an older child internationally as a single woman, which she considers one of the most difficult and most rewarding things she has ever done. She has authored adoption education materials and presented at numerous conferences and workshops throughout North America. Brooke is primarily motivated to encourage, equip, and empower parents and individuals to make changes that strengthen their lives, their careers, and their families.

Suzanne Brita Schecker, Ed.D, LMHC has practiced psychotherapy for thirty-five years. Her work is grounded in a diverse background including training in method acting, philosophy, comparative religion, Psychosynthesis, Integrative breath work, EMDR, Compassionate Listening and mindfulness-based psychotherapy.

She offers online psychotherapy and mindfulness coaching that explores basic stillness and meditation techniques that integrate the spiritual and self-help knowledge we already have. She brings the power of mindfulness to trauma recovery, grief work, adoption, and foster care, aging, couple's and family issues and difficult life transitions. All therapy is about healing the wounds of separation from our authentic self and from those we love.

Raja Selvam, Ph.D. is a senior trainer in Peter Levine's Somatic Experiencing (SE) professional trauma training programs, and the developer of the Integral Somatic Psychotherapy (ISP) approach. His background includes body-oriented psychotherapy systems of Somatic Experiencing and Bodynamic Analysis, Jungian and archetypal psychologies, and the Intersubjective and Object Relations schools of psychoanalysis. His larger understanding of the psyche is informed by his background in Advaita Vedanta, a spiritual tradition from India. He teaches extensively in Asia, Europe, South America, Canada, and the U.S.

Deanna Doss Shrodes is a licensed minister with the Assemblies of God and has served as a pastor for twenty-six years, along with her pastor-husband, Larry. They have been married for twenty-six years, have three children and live in the Tampa Bay area where they co-pastor Celebration Church of Tampa. Deanna speaks at churches and conferences internationally and is also an accomplished musician, worship leader, songwriter, and certified coach. An award-winning writer, she is also a contributing author to *Chocolate For a Woman's Courage*, (Simon & Schuster), a contributing author to *Lost Daughters: Writing Adoption from a Place of Empowerment and Peace* (CQT Media and Publishing), and the author of the book *Juggle:Manage Your Time, Change Your Life*.

Deanna blogs at *Adoptee Restoration* and contributes at *Lost Daughters* and *Adoption Voices Magazine*. She leads a search and support group, Adoptee Restoration Tampa Bay and is passionate about providing a safe place for adoptees to heal, as well as expanding the Christian community's understanding of adoption.

Corie Skolnick, M.S. LMFT was a marriage and family therapist in Los Angeles for more than twenty years, concurrently serving as an adjunct faculty member in the psychology departments of California State University, Northridge, and Moorpark College.

Her first novel, *Orfan* was selected by the prestigious Hugh C. Hyde Living Writers Series at San Diego State University (2012). *Orfan* was also a nominee for the 2012-2013 Freshman Common Reading Selection at California State University, Northridge.

Corie is a contributor to the anthology, *Adoption Reunion in the Social Media Age*, and a travel writer at the travel blog, *Desto3*.

America's Most Eligible, Corie's second novel, will be published in late 2014 by Mannequin Vanity Publishing/Mannequin Vanity Records (New York/San Diego).